ICONS

OF BLACK MUSIC

ICONS
OF BLACK MUSIC

Charlotte Greig

THUNDER BAY
P·R·E·S·S

Published in the United States by
Thunder Bay Press
5880 Oberlin Drive, Suite 400
San Diego, CA 92121-4794

©1999 Brown Partworks Ltd

ISBN 1-57145-189-7

North American Edition
Publisher Ann Ghublikian
Managing Editor JoAnn Padgett
Project Editor Elizabeth McNulty

Library of Congress Cataloging-in-Publication Data available upon request.

1 2 3 4 5 99 00 01 02 03

Picture Credits

Corbis: Bettmann 3, 9, 12, 23, 36, 63, Reuters 76, Springer 122, UPI 13, 93, 97, 100, 108, 112, 120, 136, 146; Tim Mosenfelder 118; The National Archives 70; Neal Preston 26; **Hulton Getty Picture Collection**: 8, 20, 29, 40, 45, 89, 102, 134, 135, 139, 140, 151, 154, 156, 172; **The Image Bank / Archive Photos**: 38, 47, 52, 148; CBS Television 92; Frank Driggs 16, 18, 30, 72, 74, 80, 98, 106, 130, 131, 162, 164, 165, 174; Fotos International 150, Museum of the City of New York 11; Reuters / Alexander Natruskin 82; United Artists 42; **Pictorial Press**: 10, 24, 86, 154; Showtime 123; **Redferns Music Picture Library**: Glenn A. Baker Archives 34, 90; James Barron 158; Beryl Bryden 71; Harry Goodwin 138, 160; William Gottlieb 28, 62, 88, 110; Mick Hutson 171; Max Jones Files 46; Chi Modu 142; Michael Ochs Archives 34, 66, 78, 96, 132, 170; RB 48; David Redfern 14, 19, 22, 104, 144, 152, 168; Ebet Roberts 58, 116, 126; Chuck Stewart 50; Retna Pictures: Michael Putland 61; **Rex Features**: Jack Barrow 128; **The Ronald Grant Archive**: 25; **Sylvia Pitcher Photo Library**: Sylvia Pitcher 8, 94, 114; **Val Wilmer Photography**: 32, 44, 54, 56, 60, 64, 68, 84, 124, 166.

Front cover: James Brown, **Corbis**: Bettmann.
Back cover: Diana Ross, **Redferns Music Picture Library**: Harry Goodwin.
Title page: Miles Davis, **Corbis**: Bettmann.

Printed and bound in Dubai

CONTENTS

INTRODUCTION

FROM LEADBELLY TO GRANDMASTER FLASH, from Bessie Smith to Chaka Khan, this book celebrates the great icons of black music. At the start of the twentieth century, the music of black Americans was little known outside the southern U.S. By the year 2000, however, it had taken over the world. In so doing, it had remained linked with its roots: any rock band playing a 12-bar blues riff is demonstrably descended from Robert Johnson, and the vocal style of a French singer wailing a soul song goes straight back to a southern Baptist chapel of 60 years ago.

Why did the music of an oppressed people take over the world? The answer lies in the great individuals of the music: they gave voice to a range of emotions and feelings that touched a chord in the universal human psyche. The triumph of black music is the triumph of these individuals, who produced art that was unique to them and yet appealed worldwide—the tragic intensity of John Coltrane; the cool sophistication of Dionne Warwick; the optimism of Stevie Wonder.

Some of these icons had a relatively untroubled ride to greatness. Others had to fight to create their masterpieces. Up to the sixties, segregation and racism were the background to every black artist's life, and since then the problems faced by individuals within the black community of the U.S. have remained immense. "Nobody knows the trouble I've seen" has been the recurring theme of much black music throughout the century. Even today, rap artists still reflect a harsh ghetto life of pimping, drug running, and hustling to get by. Some musicians were emotionally or physically broken by the environment they had to live in—the great tenor-sax player Lester Young never recovered from the harsh treatment he received in the army. Others, such as Charlie Parker and Billie Holiday, found solace in a world of drugs that eventually destroyed them. Artists like Dizzy Gillespie and Prince invented mysterious personas to keep the world at bay. Still others developed a tough exterior that led them to arrogance, or even physical violence—such as Leadbelly and the Notorious B.I.G.

The musical styles that these great musicians drew from developed in a southern U.S. slave culture that had its own music, often coming directly from African originals. Between the end of slavery after the Civil War and the end of the nineteenth century, a variety of influences—church music, work songs, folk ballads, African and European dances, military and marching band music—combined to create, very broadly, three streams that, although they intermingled, were identifiable and distinct.

The first of these streams was the blues, a music that reflected the concerns of people in their everyday lives. The archetypal bluesmen and women sang for nothing out in the fields, or traveled around the country as hobos, until a small-time entertainment circuit of tent shows, vaudeville troupes, and cutting contests in bars and clubs grew up, giving a few of them the chance to earn a living by playing music. But the blues offered no long-term escape from the life of hard work and oppression.

Gospel music, on the other hand, became a music that offered, at least, a better afterlife. The choral and solo singing of the black churches was a glorious affirmation of paradise to come, and the churches that featured gospel choirs produced touring bands of singers who went on to carve out great careers. They pioneered a cool, close-harmony style that has remained important ever since.

The third major strand of black music in the first half of the century was jazz, which was born in New Orleans in the years before 1917. It then spread north, and in the twenties—the "Jazz Age"—its danceable rhythms made it the major popular music in the U.S. Jazz rapidly developed beyond this stage after several great instrumentalists showed how it could become a vehicle for soloist expression through improvisation.

The story of the second half of the century is how these three strands of black music changed and interwove to create new, enormously popular forms. This process was partly fueled by the movement of blacks within the U.S. The migrations of black southern farmworkers to northern industrial cities such as Chicago and Detroit was accompanied by a change in the nature of the blues, for example. An urban blues style grew up, custom-made for the Saturday night dance hall: rhythm and blues. The music was quite literally electrified, as electric guitars replaced acoustic models. When this urban blues was put together with jazz rhythms by exuberant artists such as Fats Domino and Louis Jordan, the hybrid rapidly developed into rock'n'roll.

Perhaps the greatest coming together was that of urban blues and gospel. Suddenly, in the late fifties, gospel singing styles were being used over rough blues rhythms by artists such as Ray Charles, and soul was born. Labels such as Stax and Motown found artists such as Otis Redding and Smokey Robinson, who were masters of the new synthesis. During the sixties the sound of soul was taken up everywhere.

With barriers collapsing, the sixties, seventies, eighties, and nineties saw many and various movements in black music. Artists such as Sly Stone, Prince, and Public Enemy, for example, broke down the barriers between black music and the lucrative rock mainstream. This also opened the way for black musicians from other areas, who were able to use the U.S. as a way of bringing their national heritage to a world stage—Miriam Makeba from South Africa, Youssou N'Dour from Senegal, and Jimmy Cliff and Bob Marley from the Caribbean.

The musicians in this book span the twentieth century. Their music speaks for all humanity. They are the icons of black music.

LOUIS ARMSTRONG

1 9 0 1 — 1 9 7 1

LOUIS ARMSTRONG did more than any other artist to turn jazz into a vehicle for individual expression rather than collective improvisation. His dramatic trumpet playing, unorthodox style of singing, and natural showmanship made him the most famous jazz musician of his day. Also known as "Satchmo" and "Pops," by the time of his death, Armstrong was also held in great affection by a large public outside the jazz world.

Armstrong was born into poverty in Storyville, the red light district of New Orleans. He learned to play the cornet as a child in the Home for Colored Waifs. As a teenager, he got a full-time job playing in Fate Marable's band on the Mississippi riverboats, a good experience for him as a professional musician. He then moved to Chicago where he joined King Oliver's Creole Jazz Band, developing a duet style of cornet playing with Oliver and recording songs such as "Working Man's Blues."

In 1924 Armstrong married pianist Lil Hardin and moved to New York to join Fletcher Henderson's band, where he made his debut as a singer with "Everybody Loves My Baby." In 1925 he formed his own group, the Hot Five, switching from cornet to trumpet and developing a brilliant style of solo improvisation.

From the thirties on, Armstrong made the transition from jazzman to world-class entertainer. He toured the world with his new band, the All Stars, enjoyed a screen career in such memorable films as *Pennies from Heaven*, *High Society*, and *Hello Dolly*, and had big chart hits such as "Blueberry Hill," "Mack the Knife," and "What a Wonderful World." He also released several successful albums, including: *Satchmo: A Musical Autobiography*, a four-album review of his work, and *Louis and His Friends*, featuring guest players such as Miles Davis and Ornette Coleman. Armstrong continued to tour until 1970, a year before his death from heart failure.

ABOVE: *Louis Armstrong (left). His Hot Five in Chicago in 1925 also featured (from second left) Johnny St. Cyr, Johnny Dodds, Kid Ory, and his wife, Lil Hardin.*

OPPOSITE PAGE: *At the peak of his career Armstrong was regarded as America's greatest black entertainer.*

PEARL BAILEY

1 9 1 8 — 1 9 9 0

SINGER, DANCER, AND ACTRESS Pearl Bailey was one of the great entertainers of American show business. An uninhibited live performer, "Pearlie May," as she was known, was a big crowd-pleaser wherever she performed. During the forties, she sang with some of the most important big bands of the era, including those of Count Basie and Cab Calloway, and also appeared in musicals and films. In the sixties, she worked in cabaret, where her quickfire sense of humor won her many fans. During the seventies, she hosted her own TV show.

Bailey's family moved to Washington, D.C., when she was a child. There she won several talent contests, and started her career as a dancer, like her brother Bill Bailey. She then worked as a singer with the big bands led by Edgar Hayes, Cootie Williams, and Count Basie. In 1944 she made her debut nightclub appearance at New York's Village Vanguard, and the same year began an eight-month residency at the Blue Angel in New Orleans. She was a natural cabaret artist, setting the audience at ease with her relaxed style and throwaway remarks. She then toured with Cab Calloway, replacing Sister Rosetta Tharpe, and in 1946 appeared in the Broadway musical *St. Louis Woman*. The following year she starred in her first film, *Variety Girl*, singing the song "Tired," which became her first record.

ABOVE: *Bailey's appeal lasted throughout her career. Here she reads from her autobiography, published in 1968.*

Bailey continued to record during the forties and fifties, working with musical director Don Redman. Her best-known songs included a duet with Frank Sinatra, "A Little Learnin' is a Dangerous Thing," a comic version of Louis Jordan's "Saturday Night Fish Fry," and a pop hit, "Takes Two to Tango." In the fifties and sixties, Bailey continued her acting career in films such as *Carmen Jones*, *Porgy and Bess*, and *All the Fine Young Cannibals*. She also worked on the stage, her most notable role being the matchmaker Dolly Gallagher in the all-black musical *Hello, Dolly*. In 1968 she published her autobiography, *The Raw Pearl*.

OPPOSITE PAGE: *Pearl Bailey's natural talents on stage helped make her a big box office attraction in jazz clubs, cabaret, on Broadway, and on the silver screen.*

COUNT BASIE

1 9 0 4 — 1 9 8 4

COUNT BASIE WAS the pianist and legendary leader of a band that he formed in 1936 and which eventually outlived him in a career spanning fifty years. In its early years, the Count Basie Orchestra was at the cutting edge, featuring many great young soloists, although it later became part of the show business mainstream.

William Allen Basie was born in Red Bank, New Jersey, and was given his nickname, "Count," by a radio announcer who thought his playing as good as that of Duke Ellington and Earl Hines. As a teenager, he was taught on the cinema organ by Fats Waller, and went on to tour with vaudeville acts. He then became a cinema organist for silent movies in Kansas City, before joining the Blue Devils, a jazz group led first by Walter Page (who later became Basie's bass player) and then by Bennie Moten. When Moten died, Basie formed a new band and went on to develop a unique, blues-based style of swing, which impressed producer John Hammond. In 1936 the band got a deal with Decca, recording its theme tune "One O'Clock Jump." Early stars included Lester Young and Jo Jones.

ABOVE: *Legendary as a band leader, Basie was also a superb jazz pianist. His spare style was perfect for a big-band sound.*

During the thirties and forties, Basie's band toured black clubs and dance halls, featuring singers such as Billie Holiday and Jimmy Rushing. The band recorded for Columbia and had a hit on the black charts with "Open the Door Richard." However, once the big-band era was over, Basie was forced to reduce the size of what was by then called the Orchestra. During the fifties, the band's several line-ups recorded seminal albums such as *Count Basie Swings and Joe Williams Sings* and *The Atomic Mr. Basie.*

From 1960 the Count Basie band became one of the most popular mainstream jazz bands of the day, playing with the biggest names in jazz and recording many albums. After Basie's death in 1984, his band continued to perform; they made an album called *Long Live the Chief* in his memory in 1986.

OPPOSITE PAGE: *Count Basie, Jo Jones (drums), and Walter Page (bass) record at Victor, 1947.*

GEORGE BENSON

b . 1 9 4 3

GEORGE BENSON FIRST made his name as a gifted jazz guitarist, but later became a highly successful singer. He is one of the few black artists to have triumphed in the middle-of-the-road, "easy listening" market, where his polished style made him very successful. Some jazz fans feel that his brand of crossover soul does not do justice to his talent as a jazz musician, but Benson maintains that he wants his music to appeal to as wide an audience as possible. By any standards, his albums and live shows are extremely well crafted, providing high-class entertainment for a broad spectrum of music lovers.

Benson was born in Pittsburgh, Pennsylvania, where he spent his teenage years playing with R&B groups. At age nineteen, he joined a quartet led by organist Jack McDuff, recording for the Blue Note and Prestige record labels. Some critics claim that his 1964 album, *The New Boss Guitar*, recorded for Prestige, remains one of his best. In 1965 producer John Hammond signed him to Columbia, where he made several albums before signing with A&M records. He was in big demand as a sideman during this time, mainly for his speed and flexibility on guitar, and he recorded with many of the jazz giants, such as Miles Davis, Billy Cobham, Freddie Hubbard, and Herbie Hancock. But it was only when he moved to producer Creed Taylor's jazz-based CTI label in the early seventies that he finally found a market for his own music with the albums *White Rabbit* and *Good King Bad.*

Although he had by now established a solid mainstream jazz following for his guitar work, Benson had ambitions to become a singer. To pursue this goal, he moved to Warners, where he worked with producer Tommy Lipuma. Together they created a unique sound characterized by Benson's guitar playing overlaid by his scat singing of the identical melody. His album *Breezin'* was a hit in 1976, and featured two chart singles: the title track—an instrumental—and a version of Leon Russell's song "This Masquerade." Benson followed up with four more hit albums during the late seventies and early eighties: *In Flight, Weekend in L.A., Livin' Inside Your Love,* and *Give Me the Night.* His later albums, such as *In Your Eyes* and *Tenderly,* brought him international success as one of the greatest crossover artists of his time.

George Benson reached the peak of his career in the late seventies and eighties, when his middle-of-the-road-style albums and singles sold in huge numbers worldwide.

CHUCK BERRY

b . 1 9 2 6

CHUCK BERRY WAS one of the originators of rock'n'roll. He was the first black artist to combine elements of blues, R&B, and country music to create popular songs for the teenage market. From 1955, in the space of a few years, he produced one classic single after another, all of them featuring his distinctive guitar breaks and lyrics. His songs described, often in minute detail, the consumer lifestyle and romantic aspirations of the fifties teenager, in a style that was at once a social commentary and a celebration of youth. Although Berry's own career was erratic, his musical style was a major influence on such artists as the Beatles, Bob Dylan, the Stones, and the Beach Boys.

Berry was born Charles Edward Berry in San Jose, California. His family then settled in St. Louis. As a teenager, he spent time in reform school, and was later jailed for armed robbery. As a young man he became a hairdresser, but he continued to play music with bands in the area. In 1955 he was introduced by Muddy Waters to Chess Records in Chicago, who released his first big hit, "Maybellene." The following year, "Roll Over Beethoven" and "Too Much Monkey Business'" also became hits.

Realizing the potential of the youth market, Berry went on make his name writing and performing classic teenage odes such as "Rock'n'Roll Music," "Sweet Little Sixteen," "Reelin' and Rockin'," and "Johnny B. Goode"—all of which now form part of any classic rock'n'roll playlist—as well as starring in several films. However, in 1959 his career plummeted when he was convicted on an immorality charge concerning an underage girl employed in his nightclub. He spent a year in jail. Upon his release, Berry had more hits with "Nadine," "No Particular Place to Go," and the legendary "Promised Land," songs that he is reputed to have written while incarcerated. But after that he put out little good new material. On tour, he relied on his old songs and took a businesslike attitude to performing, demanding cash up-front before his shows. In 1972 he had his biggest ever hit with a humorous song called "My Ding-A-Ling" that did nothing for his street credit. In 1979 his career stalled once more when he was imprisoned for tax evasion. During the eighties he starred in the film *Hail! Hail! Rock'n'Roll,* which was released in celebration of his sixtieth birthday and which gave an overview of his life.

Despite the intrusion of controversy into his career, Chuck Berry "the brown-eyed handsome man" remains one of the greatest influences on contemporary music.

JAMES BROWN

b. 1928

JAMES BROWN IS A hugely influential figure in black music, both in terms of his legacy as the inventor of funk, and in his role as a black artist with full artistic and financial control over his career. Always a maverick, his triumph in bringing a unique brand of Southern black music to the forefront of American culture—without sanitizing it for a white public—continues to command respect.

ABOVE: *James Brown's explosive singing and dancing earned him the nickname "Mr. Dynamite."*

Brown was born in Barnwell, South Carolina. When his parents separated, he was raised by an aunt in Augusta, Georgia. He grew up in extreme poverty. As a young man, he spent some time in prison. In the early fifties he formed a gospel group with Bobby Byrd and settled in Macon, Georgia, signing with King Records, who released his first hits, "Please Please Me," and "Try Me."

During the sixties, Brown gained a reputation as a hard taskmaster, allegedly fining his musicians for playing wrong notes. In 1962 he became the first R&B artist to sell a million records, with his album *Live at the Apollo*. From 1964 Brown and his band, the JBs, now featuring saxophonist Maceo Parker, released such hits as "Out of Sight," "Papa's Got a Brand New Bag," and "It's a Man's Man's Man's World," all of which emphasized rhythm "on the one and three, the downbeat, in anticipation," as Bootsy Collins described it. In 1968 Martin Luther King was assassinated. Brown's response was to urge people not to riot, but at the same time he released "Say It Loud, I'm Black and I'm Proud."

The seventies marked Brown's classic funk period, backed by a new band featuring Bootsy Collins, with hits such as "Get Up (I Feel Like Being a) Sex Machine." These were later extensively sampled by a new generation of hip-hop artists to whom he responded with a rap single of his own, "Rapp Payback." In 1986 he had a hit with "Living in America" from the film *Rocky IV*. Today, despite a period of unbalanced behavior and imprisonment, Brown is still acclaimed as the "Godfather of Soul."

OPPOSITE PAGE: *During the sixties, Brown and the JBs were regarded as the most exciting live band in the U.S.*

CAB CALLOWAY

b . 1 9 0 7

CAB CALLOWAY'S FLAMBOYANT personality made him one of the major black entertainers of the thirties. He was a showman in the vaudeville style, dressing in wide and long drape jackets and huge trousers, known as "zoot suits," and entertaining his audiences with energetic song and dance routines. In a sense, he is very much a figure of his time, yet his influence on contemporary black music has been profound. Nicknamed "his Royal Highness of hi-de-ho," his hip vocabulary and scat singing style anticipated rap, while his somersaults and spins on stage prefigured break dancing.

Born in Rochester, New York, Cabell Calloway grew up in Baltimore and first sang in a group called the Baltimore Melody Boys. As a young man, he began a law course but dropped out—a more unlikely lawyer is hard to imagine. Instead, he joined the Chicago club circuit, touring with his sister Blanche, also a singer. In 1927 he appeared in the all-black review *Plantation Days*. Two years later he settled in New York and joined Connie's Hot Chocolates. The spring of 1930 saw him performing as Cab Calloway and Orchestra at Harlem's Cotton Club on Lennox Avenue at 145th Street, where live broadcasts and a hit record, "Minnie the Moocher," helped him become famous. To a general audience, Calloway's nonsensical, tongue-twisting rhymes seemed innocuous enough, and "hi-de-ho" became a national catch phrase. But many of his songs, such as "Tickeration," "Kicking the Gong Around," and "Minnie the Moocher's Wedding Day," were full of sexual innuendo and references to drugs.

During the thirties and forties, Calloway's Orchestra became one of the most popular dance bands in America, performing many of the bandleader's original songs. Their biggest hit came in 1939 with the million-selling "Jumping Jive." He also starred in several films, including *The Big Broadcast* in 1932, *The Singing Kid* in 1936, and *Stormy Weather* in 1943. At the end of the big-band era, Calloway launched himself on a career in musicals, appearing in Gershwin's *Porgy and Bess* in 1952 as the character Sportin' Life (which was based on him anyway), and in the all-black version of *Hello, Dolly*. In the eighties, he revived his career once more with performances in the films *The Blues Brothers* and Francis Ford Coppola's *The Cotton Club*.

Cab Calloway, the "Hi-de-ho-Man," was one of the most successful bandleaders of the thirties and forties. He also promoted the careers of other leading jazz musicians, such as Ben Webster and Dizzy Gillespie.

RAY CHARLES

b. 1 9 3 0

RAY CHARLES IS A prodigiously talented musician, singer, and composer, and was the first black artist to consciously fuse the blues with gospel, paving the way for soul music. During the fifties, many commentators were horrified at the way he ignored the division between the blues and gospel, blurring the lines between the secular and the religious. Nevertheless, his sound was so powerful that it managed to break down cultural barriers within black music, as well as extending into the mainstream of rock'n'roll. Not content with upending the traditions of black music, Charles also approached country music with the same lack of concern for convention: his million-selling album *Modern Sounds in Country and Western Music* of 1962 showed that, even if a white man couldn't sing the blues, a black man certainly could sing country.

Ray Charles Robinson was born in Albany, Georgia. After contracting glaucoma as a young child, he gradually became blind. He moved to a special school in Florida, where he learned jazz and classical piano. He later moved to Seattle, teaching himself to arrange and compose using braille. His first recordings in the late forties were influenced by Nat "King" Cole and Charles Brown, but after signing with Atlantic in 1952, he developed his own unique "cool" style, and went on to have a string of hits on the black charts, such as "I Got a Woman." After adding a dynamic female backing group, the Raelettes, to his line-up, he had his first big pop hit with "What'd I Say" in 1959. In the same year, he released his album *The Genius of Ray Charles*.

ABOVE: *Ray Charles plays the piano in concert in 1960.*

In the decade that followed, Charles moved between soul, pop, and country with songs such as "Hit the Road Jack" and "Georgia on My Mind." In 1965 he took a year's break to overcome his long-term heroin addiction following an arrest on drug charges. From then on he released a series of very polished, eclectic albums on his own labels, Tangerine and Crossover. In 1979 he published his autobiography, *Brother Ray*.

OPPOSITE PAGE: *Ray Charles's classic and subtle musical style helped earn him the nickname "Genius."*

JIMMY CLIFF

b . 1 9 4 8

BEFORE BOB MARLEY, it was Jimmy Cliff who brought reggae music into the international marketplace. A talented singer and songwriter, he entered the music business in the early sixties, and was part of the birth of ska, the R&B-influenced Jamaican music that would eventually mutate into reggae. By the end of the sixties, Cliff had perfected a blend of pop, soul, and reggae that resulted in his worldwide hit "Wonderful World, Beautiful People." During the seventies, he took the lead role in *The Harder They Come*, a film that introduced audiences to the tough world of the Jamaican rude boy. The soundtrack album featured many fine songs and performances by Cliff, the most memorable being the gospel-styled "Many Rivers to Cross," an anthem about the struggle of black people that showed Cliff to be a writer and singer of great depth and passion. Until the late eighties, he remained the most popular reggae star in Africa and South America.

Cliff was born James Chambers in St. Catherine, Jamaica. As a young man, he recorded for record shop owner Leslie Kong, who went on to become a key reggae producer. After a number of Jamaican hits, Chris Blackwell of Island Records began to release Cliff's records in the U.K. In 1964, Cliff moved to Britain to further his career, just as Bob Marley did ten years later.

After his 1969 success with "Wonderful World, Beautiful People," Cliff's social conscience came to the fore in his next hit, "Vietnam." He also had major success with the song "Wild World" written by Cat Stevens. Cliff also wrote reggae hits for other artists, such as "Let Your Yeah Be Yeah" for the Pioneers and "You Can Get It If You Really Want" for Desmond Dekker. By the early seventies, Cliff's status as the international ambassador of reggae was such that he was the obvious choice to star in *The Harder They Come*, a role that ensured his lasting fame as an actor, singer, and songwriter.

OPPOSITE PAGE: *Jimmy Cliff's fame in South America began in 1968 when he represented Jamaica in the International Song Festival in Brazil with the song "Waterfall."*
RIGHT: *Jimmy Cliff in a scene from* The Harder They Come.

GEORGE CLINTON

b .   1 9 4 1

GEORGE CLINTON HAS BEEN called "James Brown on acid"—a bandleader and showman who introduced black audiences to the mind-expanding philosophy of the hippie generation. Along with Jimi Hendrix and Sly Stone, he pioneered a fusion of rock and funk that celebrated the traditions of black music as well as the rebellious, irreverent attitudes of the counter-culture. Always a maverick, Clinton's surreal sense of humor and fascination with science fiction made him a cult favorite. He only briefly found a mass audience with his single "One Nation Under a Groove" in 1978, a dance-floor hit that spelled out his philosophy of a human race united in music. However, Clinton's influence on later artists such as Prince has been immense, and today his records continue to be sampled extensively.

Born in Kannapolis, North Carolina, Clinton grew up in New York, singing with doo-wop groups on street corners in the early fifties. His vocal harmony group, the Parliaments, recorded unsuccessfully for Motown, having their only hit "(I Wanna) Testify" in 1967. The following year, responding to the era of psychedelia, he formed Funkadelic, a group that combined elements of progressive rock with funk. The group released *Free Your Mind and Your Ass Will Follow* in 1970 and their all-time classic, *Maggot Brain* in 1971. In 1972 he added members of James Brown's band, the JBs, to the group, including bassist Bootsy Collins.

Clinton went on to form other bands, Parliament, the Brides of Funkenstein, the Parlettes, and Bootsy's Rubber Band, developing a philosophy of his music, called "P-Funk," which cited funk as the answer to the world's problems, and which had its own language. His lyrics, often dismissed as absurd, have always displayed consummate skill. His imagery portrays a side of black life normally hidden from white people. In the song "Chocolate City" he raps "they still call it the White House, but that's only a temporary condition." He released concept albums such as *Mothership Connection*, which yielded a hit single "Give up the Funk (Tear the Roof off the Sucker)," and mounted a "P-Funk" tour in 1977 featuring science fiction sets and costumes and a performance of funk opera. During the eighties, he recorded the influential album *Computer Games*, and he later signed to Prince's label, Paisley Park.

George Clinton was unique in black music in presenting a concept show to his audience. In 1977 he even staged the first funk opera, complete with wild costumes and theatrics.

NAT "KING" COLE

1 9 1 7 – 1 9 6 5

STARTING OUT AS a jazz pianist, Nat "King" Cole became one of the most popular ballad singers of his day, scoring 78 chart hits between 1944 and 1964. Unlike most black singers of the time, his delivery owed little to blues or gospel but had a smooth, relaxed jazz quality to it. His unique voice helped him to become one of the first black artists to cross over into the pop mainstream, with classic hits such as "Unforgettable," "Mona Lisa," and "When I Fall in Love."

ABOVE: *Cole and his trio backstage at the Palladium in London, England, before the first show of their European tour in 1950.*

The son of a Baptist minister, Nathaniel Adams Coles was born in Montgomery, Alabama, but grew up in Chicago. As a child he learned piano, and later played in his brother Eddie's group. Early in his career, he played piano in clubs, and then formed his own band in 1939. When their drummer failed to show up on a date, the group decided to go ahead without him, and found that the combination of piano, guitar, and bass perfectly suited their material. The King Cole Trio recorded on several labels, scoring a hit in 1942 with a song written by Cole, "Straighten Up and Fly Right." From then on, Cole's singing came to the fore, and the trio had several more successes such as "I Love You (for Sentimental Reasons)."

Cole then began to record as a solo artist with a full orchestra on a run of hits including "Nature Boy," "Mona Lisa," "Too Young," "Unforgettable," and "Answer Me, My Love." He also became a screen idol, appearing in films such as *Breakfast in Hollywood* and *St. Louis Blues.* In 1957 he recorded "Stardust," a version cited by its composer Hoagy Carmichael as his favorite rendition of the song. Throughout the rock'n'roll years, until his premature death from cancer, Cole continued to record in the same warm, relaxed style, and in the sixties, his smooth tone and elegant phrasing influenced a new breed of singers such as soul artists Sam Cooke and Otis Redding.

OPPOSITE PAGE: *Despite being the pianist and leader of a groundbreaking trio whose blend of jazz, pop, and blues was unique in the forties, Nat "King" Cole is remembered mostly for his smooth vocals and his romantic ballads.*

ORNETTE COLEMAN

b. 1930

DURING THE SIXTIES, Ornette Coleman pioneered a new form of jazz that was at once avant garde and rooted in the traditions of black music. Reviled by some critics, he became the *enfant terrible* of his day, but was later seen as a real innovator who had led the most important revolution in jazz since the bebop movement of the forties. Coleman himself has had little commercial success in his career, but his influence in the jazz world remains profound.

Coleman took up alto saxophone at age fourteen and went on to play in R&B bands around his hometown of Fort Worth, Texas. He then moved to Los Angeles where he worked as a lift operator while studying music theory. He formed a group with trumpeter Don Cherry, drummer Billy Higgins, and bassist Charlie Haden, improvising in an "atonal" way that was not based on standard chords. Coleman outraged the jazz establishment with his innovative and unorthodox music, and he also offended many by playing a plastic saxophone (while Cherry played a pocket trumpet) and by using very simple blues elements in his music.

The group, with several changes of line-up, made their first album, *Something Else!*, in Los Angeles in 1958, and were then signed to Atlantic Records. In the autumn of 1959, Coleman and his band played at the Five Spot in Cooper Square, New York City. They opened in a blaze of publicity and controversy, and "free jazz" was officially created. The group went on to make several important albums for Atlantic, including *The Shape of Jazz to Come*, *Change the Century*, *This Is Our Music*, and *Free Jazz*, a 36-minute improvisation featuring eight musicians. Coleman's music continued to divide the jazz world. Some rushed to embrace "the new thing," while others, unprepared for such a radical new sound, remained very skeptical.

From the sixties on, Coleman developed his approach into a theory he called "harmolodics," collaborating with musicians from different cultures, such as the Indian singer Asha Puthli and the Moroccan Master Musicians of Joujouka.

During the seventies, he formed Prime Time, a jazz-funk group that featured his son, Denardo, on drums. In the eighties and nineties, he continued his eclectic collaborations. In 1991 he was featured on the soundtrack to the film *The Naked Lunch*.

Ornette Coleman's performance in 1959 was so stunning that it has often overshadowed his subsequent work. But the love and hate he inspired rocketed him to fame in the jazz world.

JOHN COLTRANE

1 9 2 6 — 1 9 6 7

JOHN COLTRANE'S PLAYING combines technical skill with a spiritual depth that makes him one of the most powerful voices in the history of jazz. In the sixties, he became the most important jazz artist, creating a sound that was fresh, forceful, and genuinely modern. He became influenced by Eastern music and religious philosophy, releasing albums such as *A Love Supreme*, and broadened the boundaries of jazz with free-form improvisation. Sadly he died early from cancer, at age forty, but his strong, intense playing went on to inspire a whole new generation of jazz musicians. On his instrument, the tenor sax, he remains by far the single most influential player in jazz.

Coltrane grew up in Hamlet, North Carolina, where his mother played piano in church. His father, a tailor, played violin. He learned clarinet and alto saxophone, and then moved to Philadelphia. His early professional years were spent playing with a naval band in Hawaii during his military service, with Eddie Vinson's R&B band, and later with Dizzy Gillespie's orchestra. He then worked for saxophonist Earl Bostic and sometime Ellington sideman Johnny Hodges.

In 1955 Coltrane joined Miles Davis and went on to play on a series of his albums. Two years later, after many career problems up to that point because of drug addiction, he cleaned up for good. He then worked with pianist Thelonious Monk, developing a way of playing using strings of notes in a style that jazz critic Ira Gitler called "sheets of sound." During the late 1950s, Coltrane continued his association with Davis, and made notable contributions to the albums *Milestones* and *Kind of Blue*. In 1957 he recorded a classic album under his own name, *Blue Train*, which many critics see as one of his best works.

After leaving Davis, Coltrane led his own groups. By 1962 this had settled down to a quartet, with McCoy Tyner on piano, Jimmy Garrison on bass, and Elvin Jones on drums. The group played with a fierce intensity using modes and scales rather than chord changes, and this opened up new, more, free perspectives. Two classic albums were recorded with this line-up: *Live at the Village Vanguard*, on which the quartet was joined by Eric Dolphy, and *A Love Supreme*.

Coltrane himself followed up these avenues from 1965 until his death, working with musicians such as Archie Shepp, Pharoah Sanders, and his wife, Alice Coltrane.

John Coltrane pictured on a visit to London, England, in 1961.

SAM COOKE

1 9 3 1 — 1 9 6 4

SAM COOKE WAS perhaps the most perfect star black music has produced: a wonderful singer with a smooth, mellifluous voice; a handsome heart-throb who had women fainting in the aisles; and a man of great charisma and personal charm. From a gospel background, he moved effortlessly into the pop world, singing in a style that suggested, rather than emphasized, his sensuality and passion. Along with Ray Charles, Cooke was the major precursor of soul music, causing controversy in the fifties by "crossing over" from gospel to pop. However, by the time of his death, Cooke had become one of the best-loved black artists of his day, an idol who symbolized the upwardly mobile aspirations of black Americans, yet also expressed the painful reality of their lives. For many, Cooke's untimely death came to symbolize these contradictions. At the height of his career, the urbane Cooke was shot dead in a brawl with the manager of a $3-dollar-a-night Hollywood motel.

Cooke was born Sam Cook in Clarksdale, Mississippi, the son of a minister; he later added the "e" to his surname. He grew up in Chicago, singing gospel in a group called the Highway QCs, where he was discovered, at age fifteen, by J. W. Alexander of the renowned gospel group the Pilgrim Travelers. He was then introduced to the Soul Stirrers, became their lead singer, and went on to become an idol of the gospel circuit with hits such as "Jesus Gave Me Water."

It was not long before Cooke set his sights on secular music. With the support of producer Bumps Blackwell, he changed his name to Dale Cook, so as not to offend his gospel audience, and released a single called "Lovable." In 1957 he had his first hit with "You Send Me," which reached number one on both the black and pop charts. From then on, Cooke had numerous top forty hits, including "Chain Gang," "Wonderful World," "Cupid," "Twisting the Night Away," and "Bring It on Home to Me." In 1960 he signed to RCA, where his records were given a schmaltzy pop sound, but unlike most black artists of the day he continued to retain control over his career, setting up his own label, Sar, which provided an outlet for his more earthy, R&B-styled taste. His last hit was the self-penned "A Change Is Gonna Come," a moving Civil Rights anthem that reached the charts in 1965, a year after his death.

Sam Cooke, an urbane and handsome man, suffered a tragic end to a career founded on hope, love, and redemption. He remains one of the most influential singers in the history of soul music.

MILES DAVIS

1 9 2 6 — 1 9 9 1

MILES DAVIS HAS had more influence on jazz today than any other single artist. In a career spanning four decades, Davis helped to shape the music's history, beginning with his role in the creation of bebop, and continuing with a series of innovations in which he fused jazz with other contemporary musical forms.

Perhaps his most accessible record is the classic *Kind of Blue*, recorded in 1959; but there are many other aspects to Davis's talent. In the mid-forties, he played with Charlie Parker during the forging of modern jazz; in the late forties, with arranger Gil Evans, he brought the sophistication of contemporary classical music to jazz with *The Birth of the Cool*. The late fifties saw him re-enter his cool jazz phase, and in the sixties, he reinvented chamber jazz with Herbie Hancock and Wayne Shorter. In the late sixties, Davis rose to the challenge of electrifying the music with his definitive jazz-rock album *Bitches Brew*, and during the seventies went on to create jazz funk. In the eighties, he formed yet another classic group, with bassist Marcus Miller, and produced a startlingly modern funk-jazz hybrid. Davis's ability to remain one step ahead of his time earned him great respect in many fields of music, and by the time of his death, his reputation as coolest jazzman on the planet was still intact.

Davis was born into a middle-class family in Alton, Illinois, but later moved to East St. Louis. His father, a dentist, gave him a trumpet for his thirteenth birthday. After taking lessons, he won a scholarship to the Juilliard School of Music in New York, but soon dropped out of college to play and record with the leading lights of bebop, Charlie Parker, Charles Mingus, and others.

He developed an assured, minimal style that contrasted well with the fast runs played by his bebop peers. He soon began to lead his own bands, and by 1955 was being feted at the Newport Jazz Festival as a star. Although an innovator, he did not join Ornette Coleman's free-jazz fraternity, but instead pursued his own path. From the late sixties, Davis developed fusions of jazz with rock, funk, disco, and pop, all the while retaining his oblique, limpid style of playing. Davis is unique in jazz in that his development as a player is documented in his huge body of recorded work, most of which has set standards for other jazz musicians.

Miles Davis pictured in the studio in 1954, playing the trumpet with a metal harmon mute. By the early sixties, this innovation was employed regularly by jazz musicians.

ERIC DOLPHY

1 9 2 8 — 1 9 6 4

ERIC DOLPHY was a supremely talented saxophone, bass-clarinet, clarinet, and flute player, as well as a composer. He was one of the most important names of jazz when, the day after his thirty-sixth birthday, he died from a heart attack. Like John Coltrane and Ornette Coleman, Dolphy was developing a new approach to jazz, introducing Eastern tone systems into the music and pioneering a way of playing that extended the boundaries of conventional Western chord structures and melodies. As well as being innovative, his playing had an energy and verve that appealed to many jazz fans. Some critics feel that, had Dolphy lived longer, he would have matched John Coltrane as one of the greatest figures of modern jazz.

Born in Los Angeles, Dolphy learned clarinet and oboe as a child. He then played alto saxophone in big bands before joining the army in 1950. Once his military service was completed, he returned to Los Angeles and met up with fellow iconoclasts Ornette Coleman and John Coltrane before going on to join Chico Hamilton's cool jazz combo. In 1959 Dolphy moved to New York, where he began a working relationship with bassist Charles Mingus that led to a series of classic albums. In 1960 Dolphy made the seminal album *Free Jazz* with Ornette Coleman, and the following year toured with John Coltrane, recording the albums *Olé Coltrane, Impressions,* and *Africa Brass*. Dolphy had a lighter, less muscular tone than Coltrane, but his playing had a strength and passion that enabled him to hold his own in the turbulent ensembles of modern jazz. However, Dolphy also toured and recorded with his own bands. In 1961 a live show at the Five Spot in Cooper Square, Greenwich Village, in New York, was released on record to great acclaim, and his 1964 Blue Note album *Out to Lunch*, featuring Freddie Hubbard and Tony Williams, is regarded as his last great studio album.

In 1964 he toured Europe with Charles Mingus, and then played some solo shows in France and Holland. A month later, while in Berlin, Dolphy suffered a heart attack as the result of undiagnosed diabetes. Charles Mingus's impassioned performance of "So Long, Eric," written when Dolphy had left Mingus's band, was a fitting tribute to his friend's great unfinished career.

Eric Dolphy plays at a site near the venue for the 1960 Newport Jazz Festival. The festival was canceled due to the bad behavior and rioting of "college kids from out of town."

FATS DOMINO

b . 1 9 2 9

FATS DOMINO was one of the architects of rock'n'roll. His image as the rotund, happy-go-lucky black man at the piano was an archetype of U.S. culture, and he played in a long-established New Orleans tradition (also incorporating influences from boogie-woogie pianist Albert Ammons). Yet, with the advent of rock'n'roll in 1955, his style suddenly became fashionable, as white teenagers began to discover the diverse regional forms of black music that had been evolving in America since the blues. In particular, it was the cities alongside the Mississippi River—New Orleans, St. Louis, and Memphis—that produced many of rock'n'roll's greatest stars, including Domino, Little Richard, Chuck Berry, Ike Turner, and Elvis Presley.

Born into a musical New Orleans family, Antoine Domino learned piano from his uncle, jazz player Harrison Verrett. He joined Billy Diamond's band in 1945. As a young man, he had several hits on the R&B charts including "The Fat Man" before, in 1955, "Ain't That a Shame" helped him cross over from black to white audiences. The song was later a big hit for teen idol Pat Boone, setting a pattern that persisted in the music industry for many years, in which white artists performed covers of black songs in an (often successful) attempt to reach a wider market. In this case, Boone's version of the song outsold Domino's.

Despite the fact that Boone had greater success with the song, Domino remained an important figure on the rock'n'roll scene, touring with the major stars of the day, and continuing to have hits, both with original compositions and with standards such as "Blueberry Hill," "My Blue Heaven," and Bobby Charles's "Walking to New Orleans." He also appeared in several rock'n'roll films of the day, such as *Shake, Rattle and Roll* in 1956 and *The Girl Can't Help It* the following year. During the six years between 1955 and 1960, Domino had twenty Top 20 hits. During the sixties, his popularity declined, but in the seventies, he became a much-loved figure on the revival circuit, made several new recordings, and starred in the 1973 film *Let the Good Times Roll*. His popularity continued into the eighties and nineties, though his tours became less frequent. However, with worldwide sales of over 65 million records, Domino remains one of the most popular ever exponents of New Orleans' music.

Fats Domino's piano style was in the New Orleans tradition, but suddenly became popular with white people during the mid-fifties with the advent of rock'n'roll.

Earth Wind and Fire

Philip Bailey *b. 1951*   Larry Dunn *b. 1953*
Johnny Graham *b. 1951*   Ralph Johnson *b. 1951*   Al McKay *b. 1948*
Andre Woolfolk *b. 1950*   Freddie White *b. 1955*
Maurice White *b. 1941*   Verdine White *b. 1951*

Maurice White was the founder of Earth Wind and Fire, a slick funk band that incorporated elements of jazz, soul, gospel, and rock in an innovative way, and became one of the most successful groups in black music. They were classy musicians who made danceable disco music, but of a sophisticated, elegant sort that appealed to both black and white audiences at a time when racial divisions between dance and rock music were very firmly drawn. Unlike many of his contemporaries, White's music was tasteful, conventional, and unpolitical, with an upbeat optimism that made it attractive across the board. During the seventies, Earth Wind and Fire's tour with rock idols Santana established them as a crossover act, and they went on to have many pop hits, including "Shining Star," "Fantasy," "After the Love has Gone," and "Boogie Wonderland," featuring White's female group the Emotions. They also recorded Paul McCartney's "Got to Get You into My Life," which turned a pop song into a soul classic.

Maurice White and his brothers, bassist Verdine and drummer Freddie, grew up in Chicago, the sons of a doctor. Maurice studied at music school before becoming a house drummer with the Chess label. In the sixties, he toured the world with blues and jazz artists such as Ramsey Lewis and Jimmy Reed, developing an interest in Egyptology and astrology, which was later to find expression in the name and lyrics of his own band. He formed Earth Wind and Fire in 1971, going on to release the albums *Last Days and Time, Head to the Sky,* and *Open Our Eyes,* all of which sold well. Between 1975 and 1981, the group was hugely successful, releasing several million-selling singles; during this time, White and McKay also wrote the Emotions' sparkling number one hit, "Best of My Love." After Earth Wind and Fire split, singer Philip Bailey went on to record a hit duet with Phil Collins, "Easy Lover," while Maurice White continued his career as a record producer.

Mixing disco and soul to great effect, Earth Wind and Fire were hugely popular with both black and white audiences. Their classic line-up featured: (back row, left to right) Al McKay, Larry Dunn, Johnny Graham, and Andre Woolfolk; (middle row, left to right) Philip Bailey, Maurice White, and Ralph Johnson; (front row, left to right) Freddie White and Verdine White.

DUKE ELLINGTON

1 8 9 9 — 1 9 7 4

DUKE ELLINGTON commands respect as the man whose brilliance as a composer helped to create big-band jazz. In the words of his colleague, arranger Billy Strayhorn, "Ellington plays the piano but his real instrument is his band."

During his career, Duke Ellington composed a tremendous variety of pieces, but he never wrote any of them down, preferring to work the music out with his band and then record it. Many of these compositions, such as "Satin Doll," "Sophisticated Lady," and "In a Sentimental Mood" have become jazz standards. The sheer artistry of Ellington's band helped to make jazz respectable to classical music lovers and gave him a reputation as one of the greatest composers of the twentieth century.

Born into a middle-class family in Washington, D.C., Ellington studied the piano from age seven, following a path toward classical music. However, during his teens he became interested in ragtime. After writing his first composition, "Soda Fountain Rag," at age sixteen, he went on to devote himself to jazz. In 1923 he gathered together a small group of musicians, including trumpeter James "Bubber" Miley and trombonist "Tricky Sam" Nanton. These musicians, in particular, gave his band its unique "jungle" sound, developing a way of playing with mutes on their instruments to create atmospheric growls and cries. From here, Ellington expanded his band, using it as a workshop and composing in an unconventional way that combined orchestration with improvisation. Instead of writing pieces for instruments, he wrote for his musicians, and with star players in his band such as trumpeter Cootie Williams, saxophonist Johnny Hodges, and bassist Jimmy Blanton, he had a wealth of skills to draw on.

During his career, Ellington wrote over a thousand orchestrations, including film scores, ballets, musicals, and church music. But today, a number of pieces recorded between 1939 and 1941, such as "Harlem Air Shaft," "Concerto for Cootie," and "Cotton Tail," have come to be regarded as some of his best works. Many later jazz artists, including Gil Evans, Thelonious Monk, and Charles Mingus, have acknowledged Ellington's profound influence on their work.

OPPOSITE PAGE: *Ellington's compositions have earned him a reputation as one of the greatest composers of the twentieth century.*
RIGHT: *Ellington relaxes in a hotel while on tour in 1963.*

ELLA FITZGERALD

1 9 1 8 — 1 9 9 6

FOR MANY YEARS, Ella Fitzgerald was America's favorite female jazz singer. Her sweet, clear voice and wide vocal range, together with her technical skill, made it possible for her to sing in a wide variety of styles, from show tunes to pop ballads. Her jazz improvisations, or "scat" singing, became her trademark, giving even her pop material a jazz feel. Her most famous recordings were her "songbook" albums, on which she interpreted works by such writers as Jerome Kern, Cole Porter, Rodgers and Hart, and Duke Ellington. Arranged by such people as Nelson Riddle, these albums appealed

ABOVE: *Ella Fitzgerald performing for her fans with Chick Webb and his orchestra at Ashbury Park Casino, New Jersey, in 1938.*

to many non-jazz fans. She made songs such as "Love for Sale" and "Ev'ry Time We Say Goodbye" seem her own, enhancing their sophistication with her vocal skill. After a career spanning nearly six decades, Fitzgerald underwent heart surgery but continued to perform until 1993, when her ill health forced her to retire. By the time she died in 1996, her courage, as well as her singing, had been an inspiration to many.

Fitzgerald was an orphan who was brought up by an aunt in New York City. In 1934 she won an amateur talent contest and went on to sing with the Chick Webb Orchestra. The following year she made her first recording, "Love and Kisses" with Webb, and in 1938 had a million-selling hit with the song "A-tisket A-tasket." When Webb died in 1939, Fitzgerald took over leadership of the orchestra until 1942, when she began to perform solo in cabarets and theaters. She toured extensively with Benny Goodman, Louis Armstrong, Duke Ellington, and Dizzy Gillespie, as well as making recordings, mostly of pop ballads. In the mid-1950s, Norman Granz became her manager, signing her to Verve where she was allowed scope to sing a wider variety of songs, to tour extensively, and to gain a wider audience. At the same time, she appeared regularly on TV and starred in the films *Pete Kelly's Blues*, *St. Louis Blues*, and *Let No Man Write My Epitaph*, becoming one of America's best-loved entertainers.

OPPOSITE PAGE: *Ella Fitzgerald is regarded by many as jazz's greatest female vocalist.*

THE FOUR TOPS

LEVI STUBBS *b. c. 1938*
ABDUL "DUKE" FAKIR *b. c. 1938*
RENALDO "OBIE" BENSON *b. 1947*
LAWRENCE PEYTON *b. c. 1938*

THE FOUR TOPS were the ultimate Motown vocal group: their soulful, dramatic love songs were powered by the impassioned gospel singing of the unforgettable Levi Stubbs, and they deservedly had a run of big chart hits from the beginning of the sixties until the mid-seventies. Their most memorable moment was in 1966, when "Reach Out I'll Be There" stormed to the top of the pop charts. Written by the Holland-Dozier-Holland team at Motown, the single had an explosive impact, its driving beat perfectly matched by Stubbs' raw, yearning vocal. Perhaps more than any other of Motown's artists, the Four Tops embodied the transformation of gospel into pop: they retained the emotional intensity of their gospel roots yet combined it with a romanticism that was as pure, light, and melodic as the sweetest pop confection.

The four group members, who stayed together in the same line-up for over thirty years, first got together in Detroit. Calling themselves the Four Aims, they toured in the black clubs around the city—known as the chit'lin circuit—and recorded for a number of labels, including Chess and Columbia, until Berry Gordy signed them to Motown. There they were teamed with songwriters Eddie and Brian Holland and Lamont Dozier, who also wrote for the Supremes, and in 1964 had their first chart hit with "Baby I Need Your Loving." They followed this up with many more great singles, including two number ones: "I Can't Help Myself" and "Reach Out I'll Be There." They also successfully covered classics such as "If I Were a Carpenter" and "MacArthur Park." When Motown moved to Los Angeles, the Four Tops decided to split with the company, and went on to have several more hits with Dunhill and Casablanca. During the late seventies and eighties, they continued to tour and record, and with their superb harmonies and slick choreography, maintained their attraction as a live band, becoming one of the most respected groups in the industry. In 1988 they had their last big hit with the song "Loco in Acapulco" from the soundtrack to the film *Buster*.

Featuring the same line-up for more than forty years, the Four Tops create some of the most sublime harmonies in soul music. They comprise (clockwise, from the top): Lawrence Peyton, Levi Stubbs, Abdul "Duke" Fakir, and Renaldo "Obie" Benson.

ARETHA FRANKLIN

b . 1 9 4 2

ARETHA FRANKLIN, the undisputed "Queen of Soul," is regarded by many as the greatest singer in popular music. The daughter of a Baptist preacher, she grew up singing and playing piano in church. In the 1960s, she emerged as one of the biggest talents in soul music and went on to sell millions of records. Her gospel sound, songs such as "Respect," and the style in which she wore her hair and clothes, were seen as a call to black people to take pride in their identity at a time when the Civil Rights movement and the Vietnam War were causing many to question the values of American society.

Aretha Franklin was born on March 25, 1942, in Memphis, Tennessee, but grew up in Detroit. Her father, the Rev. C.L. Franklin, toured America and earned a reputation preaching fervent sermons. He brought up his five children in a strict, authoritarian manner. By age fourteen, Aretha was performing alongside her father at services and gatherings, together with sisters, Carolyn and Erma.

In 1960 producer John Hammond signed Franklin to Columbia Records. The following year she made her debut album, *Aretha*. During her time at Columbia she had some minor middle-of-the-road hits, popular with white audiences, but it was not until she met producer Jerry Wexler and signed to Atlantic Records that she realized her true potential. Wexler took her to record with musicians at Rick Hall's Fame Studio in Muscle Shoals, Alabama, giving her songs a strong flavor of the deep South and a genuine soul feel. Her first big hit on Atlantic was "I Never Loved a Man (the Way I Love You)," in 1967, followed by "Do Right Woman—Do Right Man," and "Respect," which hit number one on the pop charts the same year.

Many more hits followed, including "(You Make Me Feel) Like a Natural Woman," "Think," and "I Say a Little Prayer," but by the end of the decade, Franklin's personal life was in turmoil and she split with her husband and manager Ted White. In 1972 she made a gospel album, *Amazing Grace*, and then went on to work with producers such as Curtis Mayfield, Lamont Dozier, and Arif Mardin. In 1980 her career revived with a cameo appearance in the cult movie *The Blues Brothers*. She went on to have pop chart hits duetting with Luther Vandross, Annie Lennox, and George Michael. In 1987 she returned again to her gospel roots with a double album, *One Lord, One Faith, One Baptism*, recorded at her father's Detroit church.

In the sixties, Aretha Franklin emerged as one of the biggest talents in black music.

MARVIN GAYE

1 9 3 9 – 1 9 8 4

MARVIN GAYE HAS become a legendary figure in black music, not only because of his talent, but because of his courageous struggle to evolve from matinée idol into serious artist. One of Motown's biggest stars, he rebelled against his role as a mere product in the factory's output, creating dance music for the charts, and helped to open the way for black artists who wanted to address social, political, and racial issues in their music. However, Gaye himself was a deeply troubled man, apparently in constant conflict between the spiritual and sexual aspects of his nature, the poles of which are perhaps best represented by two of his biggest hits, "What's Going On" and "Sexual Healing." His personal life was difficult, since he was tied emotionally and financially to Motown through his marriage to its owner Berry Gordy's sister Anna, whom he eventually divorced, only to fall into a downward spiral of debt and drug dependency. In 1984 his life ended tragically, one day before his 45th birthday, when he was shot dead by his father during an argument at his parents' house in Los Angeles.

Gaye was born in Washington, D.C., the son of a Pentecostal minister. As a child, he sang in the church choir and later took up piano and drums. As a young man, after two years in the Air Force, he recorded with his vocal group the Marquees, later teaming up with Harvey Fuqua of the Moonglows. Through Fuqua, Gaye got work at Motown as a session drummer and went on to record as a solo artist before teaming up for duets with first Mary Wells, then Kim Weston, and finally Tammi Terrell. In 1969 he had a massive solo hit with "I Heard It Through the Grapevine," but the following year, Terrell died from a brain tumor while on stage singing with him, which sent Gaye into a decline. However, he returned in 1971 with the triumphant *What's Going On*, an album partly inspired by his brother Frankie's experience of the Vietnam War. The album went into the Top 10, as did three singles from it: "Inner City Blues," "Mercy Mercy Me," and the title track.

Gaye's next major album, *Let's Get It On,* was also a huge success, but by now Gaye's personal life was in chaos. He divorced Anna Gordy and did not record again until 1979, when he made *Here, My Dear* in order to pay his ex-wife alimony. In 1982, after leaving Motown, his album *Midnight Love*, released by Columbia Records, gave him his final memorable hit, "Sexual Healing."

The charismatic Marvin Gaye, pictured during a recording session in 1977.

DIZZY GILLESPIE

1917 – 1993

ONE OF THE FOUNDERS of modern jazz, trumpet player, singer, bandleader, and composer Dizzy Gillespie outlived many of the legendary figures of his time, such as Charlie Parker, John Coltrane, Bud Powell, and Thelonious Monk, and eventually became something of an ambassador for the music. This role as elder statesman of bebop tended to obscure the fact that, essentially, Gillespie was an iconoclast, more interested in breaking rules than making them. The original hipster, Gillespie sported dark glasses and a black beret in the days before this became a uniform among jazzmen, and he was renowned for his irreverent attitude and wacky sense of humor, which earned him the nickname "Dizzy."

Gillespie was born in South Carolina, where he won a scholarship to study music before moving with his family to Philadelphia. His father, a bricklayer, was also a bandleader in his spare time. Dizzy began his career as a trumpet player in the big bands of the day, including those led by Cab Calloway, Fletcher Henderson, and Earl Hines. In 1944 he became musical director of Billy Eckstine's band, which brought him into contact with Charlie Parker and singer Sarah Vaughan. During this time he also became involved with a group of musicians such as Bud Powell, Kenny Clark, and Thelonious Monk, who gathered regularly at Minton's Playhouse in Harlem, New York. Between them, they developed a fresh, fast style of jazz that became known as bebop. Gillespie went on to record many bebop classics with Charlie Parker, such as "Salt Peanuts," "Hot House," and "Night in Tunisia."

From the mid-forties, Gillespie led his own big band, touring America and Europe. But by 1950 financial constraints forced him to give up the big band except for tours specifically sponsored by the U.S. State Department. In 1954 he recorded a famous concert with Charlie Parker, *Jazz at Massey Hall*, which also featured Bud Powell, Charles Mingus, and Max Roach. Gillespie continued to record and perform with a series of smaller bands until well into the 1980s, including the Giants of Jazz, which also featured Thelonious Monk, Art Blakey, James Moody, and Sonny Stitt, and appeared regularly on Caribbean cruise ships that featured jazz artists.

Dizzy Gillespie with his distinctive upstanding trumpet. In 1953 someone accidentally fell on his trumpet, which was standing upright on its stand, and bent it. Gillespie played it and liked the sound. After that, he had his trumpets made with the bell pointing up at 45 degrees.

DEXTER GORDON

1 9 2 3 — 1 9 9 0

DEXTER GORDON'S tough tenor sax playing was an integral part of the development of modern jazz. In the 1940s, he helped to evolve bebop and became one of the seminal figures in the movement. He was a big influence on John Coltrane and Sonny Rollins, but unlike them, he continued to refine the bebop style and never moved off into the realms of the avant garde. During the 1960s, because of his refusal to espouse free jazz, he was seen as something of an anachronism, but in the seventies his style came back into favor. Equally at home on fast numbers or on ballads, his tone suggested both strength and tenderness, and he was eventually recognized as a player whose style, in its sensitivity, was timeless.

Gordon was born in Los Angeles, the son of a doctor. As a boy he played clarinet and later took up alto and tenor saxophone. He began his professional career by playing in a number of big bands, including Lionel Hampton's, Louis Armstrong's, and Billy Eckstine's. He then played with Charlie Parker, and recorded for a Los Angeles label, Dial, before fronting his own groups. Between 1947 and 1952 he took part in a series of popular saxophone "duels" in New York with fellow tenor sax player Wardell Gray. From the fifties, he recorded many albums, the most famous being 1955's *Dexter Plays Hot and Cool*. In 1962, after several spells in jail for drug offenses, he performed in London and toured Europe. The tour was so successful that he remained there, based in Copenhagen, for the next fifteen years before returning to the U.S. permanently following a successful and rewarding trip to New York in 1976.

Gordon's influence was mainly on the development of the modern tenor saxophone. He had his own unique style, based mainly on Lester Young's, but with a complex harmonic sense, and an extraordinarily laid-back rhythmic phrasing that stayed essentially the same throughout his forty-year career.

Late on in his career, Gordon starred in *Round Midnight*, a film based on the life of pianist Bud Powell, with whom he had collaborated in the sixties. His understated, melancholic portrayal of a black American jazz musician exiled in a European city— an existence that both he and Powell knew only too well—drew great praise from the critics, and remains a testament to the often troubled life of the jazz artist.

Dexter Gordon pictured in London in 1962 at the start of a tour which was so successful that he was persuaded to leave the U.S. and live in Europe. He returned to the U.S. fifteen years later.

GRANDMASTER FLASH

b . 1 9 5 8

GRANDMASTER FLASH is one of the inventors of hip-hop, the movement that arose out of the street parties of New York during the seventies. Along with Kool DJ Herc and Afrika Bambaataa, Grandmaster Flash pioneered a style of playing records that allowed an MC, or rapper, to chant and rhyme over the music. Using two turntables, Flash would cut between one instrumental section of a record to another, creating extended "break beats" as a backing rhythm for the rapper. He also developed a unique way of "scratching" records, winding the record backward and forward under the needle so that it made a percussive sound. Grandmaster Flash's innovative approach and technical brilliance made him the preeminent DJ in his field; in a sense, he was the first musician to use vinyl as his instrument. His collaboration with MC Melle Mel led to one of the most powerful rap records of all time, "The Message," a gripping evocation of the pressures of life in the ghetto. Like the doo-wop groups of the fifties, Grandmaster Flash and the hip-hop crews of the seventies were making music that came straight out of the street life of the city.

Born Joseph Saddler in the Bronx, Flash became well known in the area as a young DJ spinning records at street parties. He assembled a team of rappers and break dancers called the Furious Five, featuring MC Melle Mel, and in 1979 the group had a local hit with a single called "Superrappin'." The Furious Five were then signed to Sylvia and Joe Robinson's Sugar Hill records, releasing several singles including "The Adventures of Grandmaster Flash on the Wheels of Steel," which showcased Flash's mixing skills. In 1982 the group released "The Message," their most successful single. This featured strong lyrics about the problems of growing up in an urban ghetto: "It's like a jungle sometimes, it makes me wonder how I keep from going under," and began rap music's engagement with political and social issues. Shortly afterward, Flash left Sugar Hill and sued them over the royalties for "The Message" and the right to use the group's name. The dispute split the group down the middle, with Melle Mel siding with Sugar Hill. Flash signed to a major label but was unable to repeat his former success. However, his technical achievements had laid the groundwork for younger generations of hip-hop crews.

Grandmaster Flash and the Furious Five at the height of their success. (From left, standing): Kid Creole, Grandmaster Flash, Cowboy, Scorpio; (from left, kneeling) Melle Mel, Raheim.

AL GREEN

b. 1 9 4 6

ABOVE: *Green and his band created some of the finest soul music of the seventies.*

AL GREEN emerged in the seventies as a major soul singer and songwriter. He pioneered a smooth, subtle style of singing that was quite distinct from the raw, emotive approach of many sixties' stars such as Aretha Franklin and Otis Redding. His sensitive singing was a major influence on soul music in the eighties, as singers such as Luther Vandross presented a new image of soul as refined, sophisticated music for an emerging black middle class.

Green was born on April 13, 1946, in Forrest City, Arkansas. His father, Robert Green, was a bass player who put his sons Al, Robert, William, and Walter to work in the Green Brothers, a gospel group that toured the South and the Midwest. In 1964 Green formed a group called the Creations, later changing their name to Al Green and the Soul Mates, and had a minor hit called "Back Up Train." Green then toured with his band for several years until he met producer Willie Mitchell. Together, the pair set about writing and recording songs on their own label, Hi Records.

Hi Records was based in Memphis, home of the famous Stax label. Stax had found success partly by employing the same backing band for all their singers, thus creating a unique sound. Mitchell and Green's Hi Records followed the Stax example, maintaining a highly skilled, regular studio band that played on all of Green's records. In 1971, "Let's Stay Together" became a number one hit for Green, who went on to sell over thirty million albums during the decade, featuring hits such as "Tired of Being Alone," "I'm Still in Love with You," and "Take Me to the River."

In October 1974, Green's girlfriend killed herself after an argument, and, as a result, he quit show business. A year later, after parting company with Willie Mitchell, he began to sing gospel again. He was later ordained as a Baptist minister, and since then has released mostly gospel albums with varying degrees of success.

OPPOSITE PAGE: *Green's emotional range, sensuous but dynamic voice, and lyrics made him a compelling live performer. He is pictured here in concert.*

LIONEL HAMPTON

b . 1 9 0 9

LIONEL HAMPTON WAS one of the greatest of the early jazz vibes players. His rhythmic style of playing and his showmanship as an entertainer made him one of the most popular jazz musicians of his day. In 1930 he played vibraphone on a recording of "Memories of You" with a band fronted by Louis Armstrong. Next, he joined Benny Goodman's group before establishing his own band in 1940. Their first and best-known recording was "Flying Home" in 1942, which featured the raucous saxophone of Illinois Jacquet. Hampton's band survived, in various forms, until the mid-sixties, entertaining crowds with a mixture of swing, R&B, and sheer joyful exuberance.

Hampton was born in Louisville, Kentucky. His father died in World War I, and Lionel was sent to a Catholic school in Wisconsin, where a nun taught him to play snare drum for the school's marching band. Later, his family moved to Chicago; Hampton became a newsboy and played drums in the Newsboys' Band, learning vibraphone from percussionist Jimmy Bertrand. When he left home, he moved to California, where he made his first recordings with Paul Howard's Quality Serenaders, and sang on "Moonlight Blues." He then played with saxophonist Les Hite's band, backing Louis Armstrong. Next he was invited to join Benny Goodman's group; he stayed with Goodman for four years while also making records under his own name. During this period, Hampton recorded with such musicians as Dizzy Gillespie, Charlie Christian, and Coleman Hawkins, making some of the best swing band music of the era.

ABOVE: *Hampton at the vibes, his major instrument.*

From the forties, Hampton led his own very successful big band. Besides "Flying Home," the band had other hits such as "Hey! Ba-Ba-Rebop" and "Rag Mop" and featured many famous jazz names such as Earl Bostic, Dinah Washington, Quincy Jones, Charles Mingus, and Wes Montgomery. In the fifties, Hampton recorded with pianist Oscar Peterson, and from the sixties on, he toured Europe and Japan extensively.

OPPOSITE PAGE: *Hampton's energetic musical style was matched by an exuberant live presence, creating music that was as exciting to watch as it was to listen to.*

HERBIE HANCOCK

b . 1 9 4 0

KEYBOARD PLAYER AND composer Herbie Hancock was one of the pioneers of jazz-funk, a style that attracted the biggest audience for jazz since the swing era. During the sixties, he made a name for himself playing with Miles Davis and later recorded a number of solo albums that fused jazz with rock, disco, and hip-hop styles. Some jazz fans criticized him for making commercial records, yet Hancock continued to play and record modern jazz in concert, displaying an impressive versatility in his approach.

Born in Chicago, Hancock came from a musical family and learned classical piano from age seven. A prodigious talent from an early age, at 11 he played with the Chicago Symphony Orchestra. In his teens, he became interested in jazz and formed a band at school. As a young man, he played in trumpeter Donald Byrd's band and through Byrd, got a record deal with Blue Note. Hancock's debut album in 1963 was *Takin' Off*, which included the single "Watermelon Man." He recorded five more albums for Blue Note, and at the same time played piano in Miles Davis's group. Hancock played a crucial role in the development of modal jazz while with Davis, and was one third (together with drummer Tony Williams and bassist Ron Carter) of one of the greatest rhythm sections ever heard.

In 1968 Hancock left Davis and began to experiment with new styles of music. Like Davis, he was interested in innovation, especially in fusing jazz with more popular music and incorporating influences from Africa and India. In 1971 he released *Mwandishi* and *Sextant*, which showed him experimenting on electric keyboards. This was followed by *Headhunters*, his first best-selling album, which featured a heavy bass line and synthesizers, establishing Hancock as a leading jazz-funk artist.

In 1976 Hancock formed a small modern jazz group, VSOP, featuring members of the old Miles Davis group but with Freddie Hubbard on trumpet. He then made several disco records, using a synthesized voice effect, the vocoder, following up his chart success with an album incorporating hip-hop styles, *Future Shock*, and the hit single "Rockit," which was accompanied by an acclaimed promotional video. In 1987 Hancock won an Oscar for his soundtrack to the film *Round Midnight*.

In 1967, when this picture was taken, Hancock was nearing the end of his time with the Miles Davis quintet. Hancock's work with Davis established him as an outstanding jazz talent as pianist and composer.

ISAAC HAYES

b. 1 9 4 2

ISAAC HAYES BECAME one of black music's biggest stars during the seventies. Starting out as a backroom boy at Stax, he later launched a solo career, adopting an image akin to that of an African potentate, shaving his head and wearing a cape and dark glasses. He pioneered a new form of soul music in which long, often explicitly sexual monologues and lavish orchestration replaced the snappy three-minute R&B single, becoming one of the first soul singers to sell albums in massive quantities. He was also one of the first black artists to break into the film world, producing soundtracks such as the highly successful score for *Shaft*, which set the pattern for blaxploitation movie music at the time. With the advent of disco, Hayes's career declined somewhat, although he continued to produce records and to act in various films including *I'm Going to Git You Sucka* (1987). In the nineties, he became the voice of the chef in the cartoon *South Park*, and even had a novelty hit on the strength of this role.

Hayes was born into a sharecropping family in Covington, Tennessee. He grew up singing gospel, and moved to Memphis as a teenager, where he formed several groups that auditioned unsuccessfully for Stax. He then formed a successful songwriting partnership with David Porter and went on to pen such hits as "Hold On I'm Coming" and "Soul Man" for Stax artists Sam and Dave. He then began a solo career, using his impressively deep voice to create mini-dramas on vinyl. His version of "By the Time I Get to Phoenix," featured on the 1969 album *Hot Buttered Soul,* lasted a full eighteen minutes. Hayes continued to compose his own material but also recorded extraordinary versions of other people's work, including Bacharach and David's "Walk On By" and "The Look of Love."

In the seventies Hayes's musical career took a downturn. He left Stax in 1975 and set up his own label, Hot Buttered Soul, but was declared bankrupt the following year. His reputation was revitalized in the early nineties by British artists such as Tricky and Portishead who sampled his classic riffs. Today it is clear that Hayes was a forerunner of the rap artists of the late seventies and eighties, an original voice that acknowledged and updated a long tradition of ghetto street rhyming and brought it back into the mainstream of black music.

Bearded, shaven-headed, and powerfully muscled—Hayes's physical appearance is the perfect match for his dynamic music.

JIMI HENDRIX

1 9 4 2 – 1 9 7 0

JIMI HENDRIX WAS the first black rock star, and the most influential guitarist of his time. Having paid his dues on the road with several top American R&B bands, he moved to London in the mid-sixties and developed a way of playing that combined showmanship with dazzling technical skill and innovation. Left-handed, he played a right-handed guitar upside down, using the wah-wah pedal and the tremolo arm to control feedback noise in a style that had never before been seen or heard. In 1967 Hendrix returned to America and caused a sensation at the Monterey Pop Festival, setting fire to his guitar on stage. His albums *Are You Experienced?* and *Electric Ladyland* were groundbreaking, introducing audiences to a style of psychedelic rock rooted in the blues. His iconoclastic performance of "The Star-Spangled Banner" at the Woodstock Festival in 1969 was a revelation, suggesting that rock music could be a revolutionary medium. Sadly, only a year later, Hendrix was found dead at his flat in Notting Hill in London, having inhaled his own vomit after mixing drink and drugs.

Jimi Hendrix was born James Marshall Hendrix in Seattle. As a schoolboy, he taught himself to play guitar, listening to blues artists Robert Johnson and B.B. King. He enlisted in the paratroopers, but left two years later to tour in some of the best R&B bands of the era, backing artists such as Sam Cooke, Solomon Burke, Jackie Wilson, Little Richard, and the Isley Brothers. It was here that he learned the showmanship that later characterized his performances.

Hendrix then settled in New York, forming a band called Jimmy James and the Blue Flames, before meeting Chas Chandler of the British group the Animals, who took him to London. There, Hendrix joined bassist Noel Redding and drummer Mitch Mitchell to form the Jimi Hendrix Experience. The group quickly became part of the hip London club scene and released their first single, "Hey Joe," followed by four others including "Purple Haze" and Bob Dylan's "All Along the Watchtower." Hendrix's success in Britain helped him establish his career in America, where the music industry was then more racially segregated. He became a major star in the U.S. and set up the Electric Lady studio in New York, jamming with musician friends such as John McLaughlin and Stephen Stills. He died in 1970, just a few days after performing at the Isle of Wight Festival.

Hendrix rehearsing at the Royal Festival Hall, London, in 1967.

BILLIE HOLIDAY

1 9 1 5 — 1 9 5 9

BILLIE HOLIDAY IS REGARDED by many as the greatest jazz vocalist of all time. Like blues singer Bessie Smith, she brought a melancholic dignity to every song she sang, giving even the most superficial lyrics a depth of meaning and feeling. During her lifetime she was recognized as a great artist by jazz musicians, critics, and fans, but she never gained a mass audience.

ABOVE: *The dignity of her voice earned Billie Holiday the nickname "Lady Day."*

She was born Eleanora Fagan in Baltimore, Maryland, to teenaged parents. Her father, Clarence, a guitarist, left her mother, Sadie, shortly after Billie was born. Billie had an unstable childhood, often living in brothels, and was raped at a young age. As a teenager, she worked in Harlem nightclubs as an entertainer and began to get regular singing jobs. In 1933 record producer John Hammond got her her first recording session with a nine-piece band, featuring clarinetist Benny Goodman, at which she recorded "Riffin' the Scotch" and "Your Mother's Son-in-Law," her first two releases. In 1935 she appeared in a film called *Rhapsody in Black* with Duke Ellington and made a memorable concert debut at the Apollo Theater in Harlem. Later that year, she began to record with small jazz groups for the Brunswick label. Intended for the jukebox market, some of the songs were very ordinary, yet her phrasing and tone were unique, and she was able to make songs such as "Mean to Me," "When You're Smiling," and "I Cried for You" sound subtle yet intensely emotional.

Holiday was accompanied by such illustrious musicians as Teddy Wilson, Lester Young, Johnny Hodges, Artie Shaw, and Count Basie, but had a special rapport, both professionally and personally, with the sax player Lester Young. In the late thirties and forties, she began to perform darker material such as the anti-lynching song "Strange Fruit," as well as her own compositions such as "Fine and Mellow." Her fame grew and she appeared at large concerts and on TV, but her later years were tragic, as she struggled with drug addiction and a spell in prison. At the end of May 1959, she was admitted to a hospital in New York with heart and liver disease. She died on July 17.

OPPOSITE PAGE: *Holiday and her band perform "Fine and Mellow" in California about 1942.*

JOHN LEE HOOKER

b . 1 9 1 7

BLUESMAN JOHN LEE HOOKER's unique style and versatile approach has ensured that for over five decades he has remained a powerful voice in popular music. Since 1948, when his first hit "Boogie Chillen" topped the R&B charts, he has managed to adapt to changes in the music industry, culminating in the success of his album *The Healer* in 1989, which gave him a million seller at age 72. His gravelly voice and laid-back style hark back to the dark, elemental blues of Robert Johnson, but Hooker also adds a touch of irony and humor to his music.

Hooker was born in Clarksdale, Mississippi, the fourth of eleven children. His stepfather taught him to play guitar, and the pair performed at local fish fries. At the age of fourteen, he ran away from home to Memphis, where he met up with bluesman B.B. King. Hooker then moved to Cincinnati, and during the forties performed with gospel groups. In 1943 he formed a band that played in blues clubs and bars around Detroit, and five years later got a deal with Modern Records. He had a number of R&B hits with them, but also recorded for other companies under such names as Texas Slim, Delta John, and Birmingham Sam.

During the fifties and early sixties, Hooker recorded with a band for the Vee-Jay label, scoring hits with the singles "Dimples" and "Boom Boom." The folk revival of the period sparked an interest in acoustic blues, and Hooker reverted to a more down-home style, making albums for the folk market with such titles as *The Folk Lore of John Lee Hooker*. Soon, young white rock and blues musicians picked up on his music, and he became part of the rock scene, once more adapting to a new musical milieu. He inspired such bands as the Rolling Stones, the Animals, and Led Zeppelin, and made an album, *Hooker 'N' Heat*, with Canned Heat. During the seventies and eighties, he made a number of solo, rock-oriented albums including *The Healer*, the most successful album of his career, which featured guest artists Bonnie Raitt, Robert Cray, and Carlos Santana. This became one of the biggest-selling blues albums of all time and won Hooker a Grammy Award. In 1980 he made a cameo appearance in the film *The Blues Brothers*, and in 1986 contributed to the soundtrack for *The Color Purple*. His success continued in the nineties with the albums *Mr. Lucky* and *Boom Boom*.

Having started out as a young performer in gospel groups, Hooker has enjoyed one of the longest and most respected careers in blues music.

LIGHTNIN' HOPKINS

1 9 1 2 — 1 9 8 2

SAM "LIGHTNIN'" HOPKINS was the last in a tradition of blues minstrels, traveling storytellers who made up spontaneous songs about social issues and political events of the day. From the forties until the mid-fifties, he was a successful recording artist, but with the advent of rock'n'roll, his style lost popularity. However, when the folk revival of the late fifties and sixties took off, Hopkins was rediscovered, and he played to great acclaim at folk festivals throughout America.

Hopkins was born in Centerville, Texas, and learned his art by listening to the bluesmen around him, including his older brother Joel and the famous Blind Lemon Jefferson. He dropped out of school to travel around the state with his friend, blues singer Texas Alexander. He had many adventures, working on farms and playing in clubs; his drinking and gambling, according to some accounts, often landed him in jail. During the thirties, Hopkins settled in Houston, where he became a popular entertainer, able to improvise stories and songs at the drop of a hat about the people and places around him. In the forties, he made his first recordings for Aladdin Records, including "Short-Haired Woman," "Unsuccessful Blues," and "Tim Moore's Farm." It was at this time that he adopted the name "Lightnin'," performing with barrelhouse pianist Wilson "Thunder" Smith. Although Hopkins made many records during his career, he never earned a great deal of money, partly because he preferred to be paid cash up front rather than royalties.

In the fifties, as country blues became unfashionable, Hopkins's popularity declined. However, he continued to play in Houston, and was rediscovered by musicologist Sam Charters, who recorded his first album, *The Roots of Lightnin' Hopkins*, for the Folkways label. His tales and songs found an appreciative audience at the folk festivals of the sixties. In 1967 he was the subject of a film, *The Blues of Lightnin' Hopkins*, documenting his life and music. Hopkins capitalized on his new-found popularity. He toured Canada and the United States through the seventies, and in 1977 played in Europe. He maintained a punishing work schedule until it was curtailed by ill health, and he died of cancer at the beginning of 1982. He remains a seminal figure in the history of black music.

One of the most prolific of the Texas bluesmen, Hopkins was rediscovered as a genuine folk poet in the sixties. He was inducted into the Blues Foundation Hall of Fame in 1980.

WHITNEY HOUSTON

b . 1 9 6 3

WHITNEY HOUSTON IS ONE of the biggest stars ever to emerge from soul music. From an illustrious family of female singers, her talent and beauty were such that she became famous almost immediately after signing her first record deal. Her first album became the biggest selling debut album of all time, and she went on to score several number one hit singles, beginning in 1985 with "Saving All My Love for You." During her career she became known for dramatic love ballads such as her signature tune, "The Greatest Love of All," which showed off her powerful gospel singing and stunning vocal technique. In 1992 Houston married R&B singer Bobby Brown, a liaison that made her a natural target for the press. Later in her career she went into films, playing the part of a spoiled superstar in the film *The Bodyguard* which, although panned by the critics, was a huge box-office success. The film soundtrack featured Houston's bestselling hit "I Will Always Love You," written by country star Dolly Parton, which stayed at number one for a record fourteen weeks.

Whitney Houston is the daughter of Cissy Houston, who formed the widely respected female vocal group the Sweet Inspirations and later became a Baptist minister. She is also related to singers Thelma Houston and Dionne Warwick. As a child she sang in church, and in her teens got work as a backing singer for such artists as Chaka Khan and Lou Rawls. Clive Davis of Arista Records then discovered her and signed her up, in the hopes that her gospel style would cross over to the pop market. His hopes were more than fulfilled when her 1985 debut album, *Whitney Houston*, sold over ten million copies, followed by two more hit albums, *Whitney* and *I'm Your Baby Tonight*, both of which spawned hit singles such as "I Want to Dance with Somebody (Who Loves Me)," and "Didn't We Almost Have It All." Today some critics complain that Houston records slushy, overcommercial material far removed from her gospel roots; yet most agree that her singing remains in a class of its own.

Despite a fairly substantial break from her recording career in the mid-1990s, during which time her tempestuous marriage was highlighted by various sections of the press, Houston emerged again in 1999 with a huge international hit "It's Not Right, But It's OK."

One of the biggest stars ever to emerge from soul music, Whitney Houston is pictured in performance in 1988.

HOWLIN' WOLF

1 9 1 0 — 1 9 7 6

HOWLIN' WOLF HAS been described as a man who was larger than life, in every respect. Six foot three (1.88 m), and weighing over 275 pounds (125 kg), he had a hugely powerful voice and a menacing stage presence that mesmerized audiences wherever he went. He grew up on a cotton plantation in Mississippi, influenced by bluesmen such as Blind Lemon Jefferson, Sonny Boy Williamson, and Charley Patton, and absorbed the rich blues tradition around him. He was also influenced by white country singers such as Jimmy Rodgers, renowned for his "blue yodel"; Wolf tried to imitate this, which was how he came by his primeval "howl." During the fifties, Howlin' Wolf moved to Chicago where, along with Muddy Waters, he helped to transform the acoustic Delta blues into amplified electric music for urban dance halls. In the sixties and seventies, Howlin' Wolf and Muddy Waters were championed by white rock bands such as the Rolling Stones, performing with them at large gigs across America and Europe. By the time he died, Howlin' Wolf had become a repository of the blues tradition, interpreting a wealth of fascinating songs in his unique, dynamic style.

Wolf was born Chester Arthur Burnett, named after Chester Arthur, the twenty-first president of the United States. As a young man, he performed in small clubs around Mississippi, playing guitar and harmonica and singing with a raw and powerful voice. In the forties he moved to Arkansas, forming his own group, which included bluesmen James Cotton and Little Junior Parker. He started recording for Sam Phillips in Memphis, often under the guidance of Ike Turner. In 1951 he recorded his first hits—"Moanin' at Midnight" and "How Many More Years"—for Chess Records, and moved to Chicago, where there was a thriving blues scene. In Chicago he recorded such classics as "Smokestack Lightning," "Killing Floor," "Wang Dang Doodle," "Back Door Man," and "Little Red Rooster," songs that were later covered by acts as diverse as the Doors, Cream, the Rolling Stones, the Yardbirds, and Manfred Mann. Always a dynamic performer on stage, Howlin' Wolf's powerful act made him a familiar figure at folk and rock festivals during the sixties. He continued to perform, even when he became seriously ill, until his death in 1976.

Howlin' Wolf was a powerful presence, both in terms of his physique and his singing, which made him an exciting live performer.

MAHALIA JACKSON

1 9 1 1 — 1 9 7 2

KNOWN AS "THE QUEEN OF GOSPEL SONG," Mahalia Jackson was the foremost gospel singer of her generation. She grew up in a strictly religious environment and throughout her life refused to sing the blues, yet she had a secret admiration for blues singers such as Bessie Smith and Ida Cox, and her style was very much influenced by them. She had a beautiful, strong contralto voice, and an intense, glamorous stage presence, which unsettled the more staid church congregations she sang for. From 1955 she was active in the Civil Rights movement, traveling to Montgomery, Alabama, to lend her support to Martin Luther King's bus boycott and later singing at the Washington, D.C., rally where King made his "I have a dream" speech. At King's funeral, Jackson sang a moving version of "Precious Lord, Take My Hand"; her friend Aretha Franklin sang the same hymn at Jackson's funeral.

Jackson was born in New Orleans and, as a child, sang in the Holiness Church where her father was a Sunday preacher. There was a strong emphasis in the Holiness Church on powerful African rhythms and expressive, uninhibited singing, a style that Jackson absorbed and blended with the blues syncopations she had heard on popular records. At the age of sixteen, Jackson moved to Chicago, where she worked as a maid, nurse, and laundress. In Chicago she joined the Greater Salem Baptist Church Choir and toured in a gospel group, turning down an offer to work with jazzman Earl Hines. She made her first recording, "God's Gonna Separate the Wheat from the Tares," in 1937 and went on to sell a million records with her own composition, "Move On Up a Little Higher." Throughout her career, she continued to work, opening a beauty parlor, a flower shop, and later launching a chain of Mahalia Jackson chicken diners.

In 1954 Jackson signed to Columbia Records, recording fifteen albums for them, including *The Great Mahalia Jackson*. Four years later, she took part in Duke Ellington's gospel suite, *Black, Brown and Beige,* saying that she regarded Ellington's band as a "sacred institution" rather than a jazz band. During the sixties, she became known to a large white audience through her appearances at concerts and festivals, and on radio and TV. She continued her commitment to black causes until her death in 1972.

Jackson's glorious voice combined the styles of the Baptist and Sanctified churches with a powerful blues delivery. She is still regarded by many critics as the greatest gospel singer the world has ever known.

MICHAEL JACKSON

b . 1 9 5 8

MICHAEL JACKSON's album *Thriller* is the best-selling album of all time. Its phenomenal success made him the world's first global pop star, selling records throughout Africa and Asia as well as in the West. Jackson was also the first black star to break into MTV, revolutionizing the way in which pop videos were produced and marketed. The accompanying video to *Thriller's* title track, directed by John Landis and also starring the voice of actor Christopher Lee, was a big-budget extravaganza and remains a milestone in pop video production. It shows Jackson acting the role of a werewolf, presaging his later fascination with adopting fantasy roles.

Jackson's apparent vision of himself as a kind of alien superhuman being has given rise to a great deal of controversy, especially over his plastic surgery and skin lightening treatments, which some critics maintain is an attempt to disguise his physical characteristics as an African-American. However, it has also been argued that Jackson is attempting to liberate himself, both in his image and his music, from the constraints of race and culture, presenting himself first and foremost as a human being, and that to this degree he has been a positive role model for racially mixed and culturally displaced young people in today's world.

Jackson was born in Gary, Indiana, and from age six sang with his brothers in the family group the Jackson Five. Between 1969 and 1970 they had a series of hugely successful singles, including "I Want You Back" and "ABC." In 1971 he began a solo career and had several hits before appearing with Diana Ross in the film *The Wiz*, on the set of which he met producer Quincy Jones. Jones proved the perfect producer for Jackson, and their 1979 album *Off the Wall* yielded several hit singles, such as "Don't Stop (Till You Get Enough)" and "Rock with You." This was followed by *Thriller* in 1981, of which six of the nine tracks were hit singles, including the title track, "Billie Jean," and "Beat It." Jackson then signed a multimillion dollar advertising deal with Pepsi Cola and went on to make three more successful albums: *Bad*, *Dangerous*, and *History*. From 1985, when he co-wrote "We Are the World" with Lionel Richie for the U.S.A. for Africa charity, Jackson has attempted to introduce serious social and ecological concerns into his music, but his sincerity was called into question in the nineties by his ever more grandiose self-image and increasingly bizarre private life.

Jackson performing in Moscow in 1976 as part of his "History" world tour.

Cordially Yours
Blind Lemon Jefferson

BLIND LEMON JEFFERSON

1 8 9 7 — 1 9 2 9

BLIND LEMON JEFFERSON was one of the first country bluesmen to make popular recordings, particularly of his own songs. He had his own unique, idiosyncratic style of guitar playing and singing, with a much more fluid rhythmic approach to the blues than most of his contemporaries. During his lifetime he became the biggest selling artist in the genre. His style inspired many other blues performers, including Leadbelly and Lightnin' Hopkins, and he has been cited as a seminal influence by a later generation of blues and jazz artists, from Louis Armstrong to B.B. King. His repertoire of songs is well known outside the world of blues, especially in country and folk music.

Jefferson was born blind and his early years were lived in poverty. His blindness made him unable to find work as a farmhand, so he turned to music. As a teenager, he traveled around east Texas as a singing beggar, performing at parties, on the streets, and in bars and brothels. Later he visited most of the southern states, at one point teaming up with blues singer Leadbelly, though he always maintained links with Texas. His first recordings were of religious songs under his real name of Deacon L. J. Bates, but it was his blues songs that found popularity. Between 1926 and his death in 1929, he recorded over a hundred recordings, mostly for Paramount Records based in Chicago. His second release for Paramount, "Got the Blues," reached a large audience, and he went on to write a number of songs that became classics, such as "Black Snake Blues," "Pneumonia Blues," "Matchbox Blues," and "See That My Grave Is Kept Clean," which was recorded by Bob Dylan on his debut album in 1962.

Jefferson enjoyed success during his career; at one point he owned two cars and employed a chauffeur to drive him. He died, in mysterious circumstances, of exposure on the streets of Chicago during a snowstorm in December 1929. It is not entirely clear how he died, but it is thought that he may have had a heart attack. His body was taken back to Texas to be buried.

Jefferson's recordings continued to be released after his death. They have been compiled by Milestone Records on albums entitled *Blind Lemon Jefferson, Immortal,* and *Black Snake Moan,* and by Biograph Records on *Master of the Blues.*

The only known photograph of Blind Lemon Jefferson, taken from a Paramount publicity shot, shows him as a round-faced, youthful man in clear spectacles.

ROBERT JOHNSON

1 9 1 2 — 1 9 3 8

LEGEND HAS IT that Robert Johnson, a poor black sharecropper from Mississippi, acquired his formidable talent by going down to the crossroads and selling his soul to the devil so he could play guitar and sing the blues. Certainly, Johnson's eerie voice and chilling songs such as "Hellhound on My Trail," "Me and the Devil Blues," and "Love in Vain" seem influenced as much by ideas of black magic and African voodoo as by traditional Christianity. In fact, very little is known about Johnson's life, and it is often difficult to distinguish between the fact and the legend. For many, he personifies the blues tradition: a hobo who traveled around America, singing songs that expressed the elemental pain and fear, not only of his own life, but also of the human condition.

Johnson was born in Hazlehurst, Mississippi, into a large family. In his teens he learned to play the harmonica and the guitar, influenced by bluesmen such as Eddie "Son" House, Charley Patton, and Willie Brown. As a young man, he traveled widely around his home state, playing in the street, and at house parties, juke joints, and lumber camps. He also visited Arkansas, Texas, and Tennessee, as well as traveling to Chicago and New York. During this time, Johnson encountered many other blues musicians, including Sonny Boy Williamson II and Howlin' Wolf.

Between 1936 and 1937, Johnson made a legendary series of recordings in the back room of an office building in Texas. At the time, only one song from the sessions, "Terraplane Blues," sold any copies, but it is these recordings that now form the basis of his reputation. When producer John Hammond heard them in 1938, he immediately tried to book Johnson for a black music concert at Carnegie Hall, only to find that Johnson was dead. If Johnson's life was mysterious, so was his death. Some think that he was poisoned after drinking strychnine-laced whiskey in a juke joint or that he was stabbed by a jealous husband; still others believe that his death was to do with the black arts. Whatever the truth, Johnson's influence has been profound. His songs were recorded by a whole range of bluesmen such as Muddy Waters and Elmore James and by a later generation of rock musicians such as Eric Clapton and the Rolling Stones. In 1990 a complete set of Johnson's recordings was released by the Gold Collection that go some way to explaining his legendary reputation.

The darkness of Johnson's voice, his haunting guitar technique, and his frank songs of paranoia and despair gave rise to the legend that he had "sold his soul to the devil" for his musical skills.

LOUIS JORDAN

1 9 0 8 — 1 9 7 5

ABOVE: *Jordan the saxophonist, pictured in 1970.*

LOUIS "JUMP" JORDAN was the most important forerunner of rhythm and blues, and indirectly of rock'n'roll. A saxophonist, singer, and bandleader, he was a great entertainer who took the blues and added a dash of swing to it, creating a music that was full of life and humor. With his band the Tympany Five, which normally included a larger number of musicians, he became an enormously popular act in the forties, with million-selling pop hits such as "Is You Is or Is You Ain't My Baby" and "Choo Choo Ch'Boogie." Here was jazz that celebrated the joys of a night out on the town, drinking, dancing, and having fun, with songs such as "Let the Good Times Roll" and "Saturday Night Fish Fry." Not only were Jordan's "jump jive" rhythms a huge influence on the electric sound of urban rhythm and blues, but he also prefigured early rock'n'rollers such as Chuck Berry and Bill Haley. Berry's humorous narrative songs owed more than a small debt to Jordan, and Jordan's producer Milt Gabler went on to work with Haley, modeling the Comets' sound closely on Jordan's.

Jordan was born in Brinkley, Arkansas, and learned saxophone from his father. As a teenager, he joined a vaudeville show, the Rabbit Foot Minstrels, and supported blues singers including Ma Rainey and Bessie Smith. In the thirties, he moved to New York where he played in various big bands. In 1938 he formed his own group, the Tympany Five. They enjoyed moderate success with recordings of "Knock Me a Kiss" in 1942 and "Five Guys Named Moe" in 1943. In 1944 Jordan had his first major hit with "G.I. Joe," earning him the title "King of the Jukeboxes." He went on to sing with some of the greatest stars of the day, including Bing Crosby, Ella Fitzgerald, and Louis Armstrong. During the fifties and sixties, Jordan's thunder was stolen by rock'n'roll acts such as Haley, but he continued to entertain appreciative audiences until his death from a heart attack in 1975.

OPPOSITE PAGE: *Jordan (at the right of the picture) with his band. The humorous content of Jordan's songs never detracted from his or his band members' skilled musicianship.*

CHAKA KHAN

b . 1 9 5 3

A SOUL SINGER with the raunchy glamor of a rock star, Chaka Khan was one of the great female voices of the seventies and eighties. Her group, Rufus, followed in the footsteps of Sly and the Family Stone, mixing soul and funk with rock, and gaining a large audience outside the world of black music. Today, her hits "I'm Every Woman" and "Ain't Nobody" remain classics of funk rock.

Born in Great Lakes, Illinois, Yvette Marie Stevens grew up on Chicago's South Side, forming a group, the Crystalettes, at age eleven. As a teenager, she sang in local nightclubs, adopting the African name Chaka Khan when she worked with the Black Panthers on a welfare program. In 1971 she joined a white group called American Breed, replacing their lead singer Paulette McWilliams. The same year, the group changed its name to Rufus and released their debut single, "Whoever's Loving You Is Killing Me." Rufus went on to have nine more hits during the seventies, including Stevie Wonder's "Tell Me Something Good," Ashford and Simpson's "You Got the Love," and the million-selling "Sweet Thing."

In 1978 Khan launched her solo career with the album *Chaka*, on which she was backed by a host of quality musicians such as Randy Brecker of the Brecker Brothers, the Average White Band, and jazz guitarist Phil Upchurch, and had a smash hit with another Ashford and Simpson composition, "I'm Every Woman." She then began to experiment with other musical genres, recording with Ry Cooder (on the album *Bop Til You Drop*), George Benson (on the single "We Got the Love"), and even Rick Wakeman. In 1981 she recorded *Echoes of An Era* on which she played with leading jazz musicians such as Chick Corea and Stanley Clarke, showing that she was equally at home with soul, rock, and jazz material. In 1983 she recorded once more with Rufus, scoring a huge success with "Ain't Nobody." She then went on to work with Melle Mel and Stevie Wonder on "I Feel for You," a song written by Prince.

During the rest of the eighties and early nineties, Chaka Khan continued to make albums, working with major producers such as Quincy Jones on a variety of musical projects, as well as backing artists such as Robert Palmer (on the hit single "Addicted to Love"), David Bowie, and Steve Winwood, both on tour and in the studio.

Chaka Khan's beautiful voice and flexible attitude to music allowed her to record jazz, soul, and rock music to great effect during the eighties.

B.B. KING

b . 1 9 2 5

ONE OF THE GREAT bluesmen of the century, B.B. King created his own unique style as a guitarist and singer, combining elements of the Delta blues with jazz styles and the dance beat of R&B. During the 1960s, he was a major influence on rock guitarists such as Eric Clapton. King is known as one of the hardest-working artists in show business, with a career spanning nearly four decades.

B.B. King was born Riley B. King on September 16, 1925, in Itta Bena, Mississippi. He came from a poor plantation family, his parents separated when he was four, and his mother died when he was eight. As a boy, King sang in church and at age fifteen took up guitar. After completing his army service, he moved to Memphis and got work singing commercials on a black radio station, WDIA. Soon he had his own show under the name of "Riley King, the Blues Boy from Beale Street" (later shortened to B.B.) In 1949 he began to record, and two years later had his first number one hit on the black music charts, "Three O'Clock Blues," a song recorded at the Memphis YMCA. This success led to concert dates as far away as the Apollo Theater in Harlem. Over thirty more R&B hits followed. His famous guitar is named Lucille, reputedly after a fight between two men over a woman of the same name at one of his concerts. The fight resulted in a serious fire from which King rescued his precious instrument. B.B. King constantly toured the black clubs of America, playing 342 one-night dates in 1956 alone, and surviving eighteen car crashes.

During the sixties, his live performances and albums, such as *Live at the Regal* and *Blues Is King,* began to reach a wider market as white audiences started to acknowledge the blues as the origin of rock music. In 1969 his single, "The Thrill is Gone," reached the pop charts, giving King the opportunity to work in film and on TV. During the seventies and eighties, he continued to record his own material, also collaborating with musicians such as Taj Mahal, Bobby Bland, and U2, while remaining a hugely popular live entertainer in his own right. Having released some 70 albums, owning a string of nightclubs, and still playing more than 200 shows a year, King remains the blues' greatest international ambassador and, more than anyone else, deserves to be called "the King of the Blues."

King's live shows are legendary and some critics believe that his Live at the Regal *album, recorded in 1962, is the best blues album ever made.*

GLADYS KNIGHT

b . 1 9 4 4

GLADYS KNIGHT HAS had one of the longest careers in soul music. As a child, she shot to fame at age seven, when she won the *Ted Mack Amateur Hour*, a television talent contest. As the first black girl to win the show, she became something of a role model for a generation of aspiring African-American performers, and later described in her autobiography how people still recognize and remember her from that occasion. Together with her group, the Pips, featuring her brother Merald "Bubba" Knight and her cousins William Guest and Edward Patten, they became one of the most successful soul groups in black music history, releasing such classic hits as "Midnight Train to Georgia," "On and On," and "The Way We Were," and touring America and Europe for over four decades.

Knight was born and grew up in Atlanta, Georgia. From her earliest years, her family and friends were aware that she had an extraordinary natural talent as a singer. From age five, she toured in a church group and won various talent competitions. She then organized an informal family group, the Pips, and performed at local functions before going out on the road at age twelve, opening for acts such as Jackie Wilson and Sam Cooke. The group's first release, "Every Beat of My Heart," was a hit for them in 1961. After a stint on the Maxx label with producer Van McCoy, the Pips signed to Motown, where they went on to have many hits, including the original release of the Norman Whitfield/Barrett Strong song "I Heard It Through the Grapevine" and "If I

Were Your Woman." During the seventies, the group left Motown and signed to the Buddah label, releasing the album *Imagination,* which yielded several hit singles. In 1989 Knight sang the theme to the James Bond movie *Licence To Kill,* and the following year released her first solo album, *Good Woman.*

OPPOSITE PAGE: *In 1974 Gladys Knight was at the height of her fame.*
RIGHT: *A publicity shot of Gladys Knight and the Pips taken in 1973, just after they had signed for Buddah Records.*

LEADBELLY

1 8 8 9 — 1 9 4 9

LEADBELLY's turn-of-the-century repertoire of ballads, blues, dance tunes, and children's songs is a rich treasury of material that draws from many traditions within American rural music, both black and white. As well as giving us a picture of that period, songs such as "Goodnight Irene" and "Cotton Fields" have also helped to form the basis of today's popular music.

ABOVE: *Leadbelly was twice let out of prison because of his musical ability.*

Leadbelly was the nickname of Huddie Ledbetter, born in Mooringsport, Louisiana. As a child, he learned accordion from his uncle, and later picked up guitar and harmonica. He became a migrant worker in his teens, traveling across the country and playing with bluesmen such as Blind Lemon Jefferson, whose guitar style influenced him greatly. A big man with an explosive temper, Leadbelly spent several years in jail for murder and assault. It was while in prison that he was "discovered" by folklorist John Lomax, who recorded his songs, including several pleading for his release. In 1934 Leadbelly was released into Lomax's care, and went to live in New York. Lomax then published *Negro Folk Songs As Sung by Leadbelly*, a song collection that included a guitar tutor and a biography.

In New York, Leadbelly became allied to a left-wing group that included such musicians as Brownie McGhee, Woody Guthrie, Sonny Terry, and Pete Seeger. He toured with them on the college circuit, in clubs, and at political rallies. He also recorded extensively for the Library of Congress, and for companies such as Victor, Capitol, and Folkways. Later he moved to Hollywood and appeared in a short film called *Three Songs by Leadbelly*. In 1949 he traveled to France and performed at the Paris Jazz Fair, but toward the end of that year he contracted a muscular disease and died.

Leadbelly's songs were made known to a wider public through Pete Seeger, whose version of "Goodnight Irene" was a hit for his group the Weavers in 1948. In Britain Lonnie Donegan kicked off the skiffle movement with a Leadbelly song, "Rock Island Line," which became a Top 10 hit in 1956. Since then, many artists, from Bob Dylan to Bruce Springsteen, have paid tribute to Leadbelly by recording his songs.

OPPOSITE PAGE: *Leadbelly had a wide repertoire of blues, folk songs, spirituals, and ballads.*

LITTLE RICHARD

b . 1 9 3 5

LITTLE RICHARD WAS the most flamboyant of all the early rock'n'roll stars, both in his image and in his music. Wearing make-up and outrageous clothes, he shrieked his way through apparently nonsensical songs such as his first hit, "Tutti Frutti," which started with the word "Awopbopaloobopawopbamboom!," electrifying audiences with his manic stage presence. However, Richard's roots were in the southern Pentecostal church, and throughout his career he was in deep conflict about his sexuality and his attraction to the "devil's music." He periodically repented his ungodliness and returned to the church, singing gospel and preaching around the country, only to succumb time and again to the lure of rock'n'roll.

Born in Macon, Georgia, Richard Wayne Penniman was one of twelve children. Although his family were deeply religious, his father also sold bootleg whiskey. As a child, Richard learned piano and sang, but by age fourteen he left home to join a medicine show. He became well known in black vaudeville, modeling his style on those of two contemporaries, Billy Wright and Eskew Reeder, otherwise known as Esquerita. Wright was a blues singer who wore make-up and wild clothes, while Esquerita was an R&B artist from New Orleans who played piano in a particularly crazed, intense fashion.

In 1952, when his father was shot dead, Richard took over as the family breadwinner, forming a band called the Tempo Toppers. He had little success until 1955, when he recorded "Tutti Frutti" for Specialty Records, cleaning up the suggestive lyrics. The song was covered by Pat Boone, and later by Elvis Presley and the Beatles.

Richard went on to have such major hits as "Long Tall Sally," "Lucille," and "Good Golly, Miss Molly," touring America and Europe constantly until, in 1958, he decided to give up rock'n'roll and turn to God. He studied at Bible college and released gospel records, but later returned to the rock fold, recording "Bama Lama Bama Lou" in 1964. Although he made several new albums in the seventies and eighties, it is as a performer of his early hits that he still remains in demand. His influence on rock music has been immense: the Rolling Stones, the Beatles, David Bowie, and Jimi Hendrix (who for a short time was in his band) all learned a great deal from his repertoire, his stagecraft, and his general attitude of irreverent exuberance.

Little Richard and his band playing live for the cameras in 1957.

MIRIAM MAKEBA

b . 1 9 3 2

BORN IN A TOWNSHIP outside Johannesburg, Miriam Makeba became South Africa's best-known international singer, introducing Western audiences to the Xhosa and Zulu songs of her childhood. Throughout her career she was a staunch supporter of the anti-apartheid movement, and for many years her records were banned in her home country. For much of her life she lived in the United States, becoming a very popular entertainer there, but when she married black activist Stokely Carmichael (the second of five husbands), her career declined and she left America, moving first to Guinea, and then to Belgium. She continued to publicly oppose apartheid until, in 1990, she was permitted to return to South Africa.

Makeba's father was Swazi and her mother Xhosa. The family lived in a segregated area, Prospect Township, and as a child Zenzile, as she was then called, sang in the school choir and helped her mother as a cleaner. She learned the Xhosa language, with its characteristic "clicking" sounds, which she later used in performing her famous piece, "Click Song." From 1954 she toured as a professional singer with the vocal group the Black Manhattan Brothers, also singing with many other leading South African musicians. She specialized in mbaqanga, a type of African jazz, and formed her own female vocal group, the Skylarks. By the end of the decade, she was well known in South Africa, starring in an anti-apartheid film, *Come Back Africa*, and a musical show about a boxer, *King Kong*, which toured Europe and America. With the help of Harry Belafonte, she settled in New York, giving concerts and recording for RCA and Reprise. In 1963 she came to political prominence in the U.S. by giving a passionate speech to the United Nations explaining what life was like under the apartheid regime. In return for this the South African government took away her citizenship. But in 1967 she had a hit with the single "Pata Pata," and her career in the U.S. began to develop. This continued until her marriage to the black activist Stokeley Carmichael in 1968, which alienated members of the music business and the public at large.

During the seventies, she released several albums, and in 1987 toured with Paul Simon and her first husband, trumpeter Hugh Masekela, following the release of Simon's hit album *Graceland* on which they both performed.

A champion of African causes, Miriam Makeba is well known across the continent. Here she is at ringside before the Muhammad Ali–George Foreman fight in Kinshasa, Zaire, in 1974.

BOB MARLEY

1 9 4 5 — 1 9 8 1

BOB MARLEY was responsible for bringing the music of Jamaica to an international audience. A singer and songwriter of great power and depth, he was also a charismatic personality with a strong vision of how black people could liberate themselves from the heritage of slavery through Rastafarianism. During his lifetime, he involved himself in Jamaican political life and lent his support to the newly independent nations of Africa. Such was his popularity in Jamaica that, when he died, he was given a state funeral.

Marley was born of mixed-race parentage in St. Anns, and in 1957 moved to Trench Town, the ghetto area of Kingston. This was a poor, crime-ridden part of the city where unemployment was high and gangs of youths known as "rude boys" roamed the streets. Marley, himself sensitive and thoughtful, spoke for this generation through his music. In 1960 he formed a vocal group with his friends Bunny Wailer, Neville O'Riley Livingston, and Peter Tosh. Two years later, they cut their first hit single "Judge Not," and went on to record over twenty more hits for producer Coxsone Dodd. In 1967 they split from Dodd after a dispute over unpaid royalties. But Marley's songs were also popular with other artists, such as Johnny Nash, whose version of "Stir It Up" was a Top 20 hit in 1973.

The group, now known as the Wailers, also recorded a strongly political set of songs with legendary producer Lee Perry and his seminal house band, the Upsetters. "Trench Town Rock," released in 1971, became a huge hit in Jamaica, and Chris Blackwell signed the band to Island Records. Bob Marley and the Wailers' first album in 1972, *Catch a Fire*, launched them on a touring career, and during the decade they went on to release a string of successful albums including *Burnin', Natty Dread, Live at the Lyceum, Rastaman Vibration,* and *Exodus.* Marley's fame reached a peak in the mid-seventies when his "I Shot the Sheriff" was a worldwide hit for Eric Clapton and "No Woman No Cry" became the biggest reggae hit song ever released.

In 1976, in an attempt to calm the violence of that year's elections, Marley organized a "Smile Jamaica" concert to reconcile the warring parties. The same year, he was shot and wounded by unknown attackers. In 1980 he performed at the independence celebrations in Zimbabwe. Later that year, he was found to have cancerous cells in his toe. Despite treatment he died of cancer the following year.

Bob Marley was the only true worldwide reggae superstar.

CURTIS MAYFIELD

b . 1 9 4 2

CURTIS MAYFIELD is one of the most inspiring figures in black music. As lead singer of the Impressions, he wrote songs that recognized and celebrated black consciousness; and as a solo artist his work, like that of Marvin Gaye and Stevie Wonder, gave soul music a strong political edge. His greatest commercial success came in the seventies with the soundtrack to the blaxploitation film *Superfly*, with songs such as "Freddie's Dead" that managed to evoke the sadness and squalor, as well as the glamor, of ghetto life. In August 1990 Mayfield had a serious accident when a lighting rig fell on him during an outdoor concert in Brooklyn, New York, paralyzing him for life. Against all the odds, Mayfield has fought back, continuing to release material even though doctors predicted that he would never sing again.

Mayfield was born in Chicago, where he grew up singing in vocal groups (the Alphatones and the Roosters) with his friend Jerry Butler. In 1958, as Jerry Butler and the Impressions, the group had its first hit with "For Your Precious Love." Butler then left for a solo career. Three years later, the Impressions had almost disbanded when they had a Top 20 hit with "Gypsy Woman," featuring Mayfield's high, sweet lead vocal. A string of hits followed, including "Keep On Pushing" and "People Get Ready," songs that drew on Mayfield's gospel heritage and expressed the optimism of the Civil Rights movement at the time.

In 1968 Mayfield set up his own Curtom label, with "Move On Up" as his debut solo release. As well as pursuing his solo career, Mayfield produced numerous other Chicago acts and wrote film soundtracks, the most successful of which was *Superfly* in 1972. Later albums such as *There's No Place Like America Today* were less commercially successful but continued to provide Mayfield's trademark combination of optimism and incisive social commentary. In the late seventies, Curtom hit financial difficulties and Mayfield recorded for several different labels. In 1982 he recorded the album *Honesty*, which included "Dirty Laundry," a powerful song about the American political system. Interest in his music continued to grow until his tragic accident.

Despite being paralyzed from the neck down, Mayfield released a new album, *New World Order,* in 1996 to great acclaim.

Guitarist, singer, songwriter, and producer, Curtis Mayfield has been a huge influence on soul music for more than forty years.

MEMPHIS MINNIE

1 8 9 7 – 1 9 7 3

"THAT WOMAN WAS TOUGHER THAN A MAN. No man was strong enough to mess around with her. She was a fighter." Thus musician Homesick James Williamson paid tribute to Memphis Minnie, the only country blueswoman of her time to compete on equal terms with her male peers. Unlike other female singers of the time, Memphis Minnie was a skilled instrumentalist who regularly beat rivals such as Big Bill Broonzy and Muddy Waters at cutting contests in Chicago clubs. She was also, by all accounts, a glamorous woman with very dark skin and very white teeth, who wore high-heeled shoes and bracelets made of silver dollars. Her most memorable songs, such as "Bumble Bee," "Nothing in Rambling," "Me and My Chauffeur," and "Hustlin' Woman Blues," drew vividly on her own experiences, but she also celebrated events of the day with compositions such as "When the Levee Breaks," about the Mississippi flood of 1927, and "He's in the Ring," celebrating the success of champion boxer Joe Louis.

Memphis Minnie was born Lizzie Douglas in Algiers, Louisiana, and started playing banjo and guitar as a child. By her teens, she was playing on street corners in Memphis, in the bars on Beale Street, and traveling around the South in tent shows and circuses. In 1929 she met up with Kansas Joe McCoy, who became her second husband, and the pair toured and recorded together, eventually settling in Chicago. She left him ten years later and took up with Ernest Lawlars, known as "Little Son Joe," once again forming a musical partnership.

During the thirties and forties, her tough, urban blues sound and vibrant personality earned her great respect on the Chicago music scene. Her regular "Blue Monday" parties at Ruby Lee Gatewood's Tavern were very popular. She was a good songwriter and a gritty singer, but her real skill was as a guitarist. Big Bill Broonzy said of her that she could "Pick up a guitar as good as a man…make a guitar cry, moan, talk, and whistle the blues." But despite her talent and her determination to take her place alongside bluesmen such as Muddy Waters and Howlin' Wolf, she failed to get the recognition she deserved, retiring from the music scene many years before her death. She was ahead of her time, and it is only today that her impact is being reassessed.

Memphis Minnie's skill as a guitarist made her stand out in the Chicago blues scene of the thirties and forties. She earned her tough reputation by taking on men at what was considered their instrument—the guitar.

CHARLES MINGUS

1 9 2 2 — 1 9 7 9

BETWEEN THE FIFTIES AND THE SEVENTIES, composer, bassist, bandleader, and pianist Charles Mingus helped shape modern jazz. Today he is recognized as one of the most important black composers of the twentieth century. His orchestrations, like those of Duke Ellington, expressed a powerful historical, political, and artistic vision; yet he also emphasized the personal, allowing himself and his musicians great scope for free improvisation and self-expression. He was involved with all the great jazz movements of his lifetime, from the New Orleans style of Kid Ory and Louis Armstrong, to the big-band swing of Lionel Hampton and Duke Ellington, and the modern sound of bebop exemplified by Charlie Parker and Bud Powell. He was a passionately creative man who sought out all the best musicians of his day, working with them on ambitious suites of music that were both conceptually original and full of exciting solos.

Mingus's personal life was turbulent, but he constantly struggled to make sense of his psychological makeup, once asking his analyst to write the sleeve notes for an album. His autobiography, *Beneath the Underdog*, published in 1971, is an honest self-portrait, focusing on the sexual obsessions of his personal life rather than on the triumphs of his music, and is a disturbing yet powerful testament to a highly complex artist.

Mingus was born in Nogales, Arizona, the son of a sergeant in the U.S. Army. His mother died soon after his birth, and as a child he was subjected to beatings from his father. The family moved to Watts, Los Angeles, where Mingus learned trombone and cello, switching to bass in order to join the school band. His first records were with Louis Armstrong's band, and he also wrote and played for Lionel Hampton's band, before joining the "cool jazz" trio headed by Red Norvo. In 1951 Mingus moved to New York, where he played with many great musicians, including Charlie Parker, Bud Powell, Dizzy Gillespie, Max Roach, and Eric Dolphy. During this time he also released several innovative albums, including *Pithecanthropus Erectus*, a suite designed to trace human evolution, *Blues and Roots* with Eric Dolphy, and *Mingus Ah Um*, which featured his famous tribute to Lester Young, "Goodbye Pork Pie Hat." During the seventies, despite failing health, Mingus continued to write music and enjoyed a new status as a result of the success of his biography. He also collaborated on an LP with Joni Mitchell, but died of Huntington's chorea during the project.

Bassist, bandleader, and composer Charles Mingus was an important figure in modern jazz.

THELONIOUS MONK

1 9 1 7 — 1 9 8 2

THELONIOUS MONK was a highly influential pianist and composer, whose sparse, minimalist style of playing and unusual melodic and rhythmic structures laid the foundations for a later generation of jazz musicians. During the forties, he performed at Minton's Playhouse on West 118th Street in Harlem, New York, but it was not until the late fifties that the advanced nature of his compositions was fully recognized. He introduced unusual, sometimes dissonant harmonies into his work, often playing in a humorous style that disguised the complexity of his music. Monk composed a number of songs that went on to become jazz standards, including "Straight, No Chaser," "Round About Midnight," "Blue Monk," and "Epistrophy."

Monk grew up in New York, and started to play piano at age eleven, accompanying his mother in church. He was influenced by the jazz piano of Fats Waller, Earl Hines, and Art Tatum, and began his career playing at rent parties, raising money for poor neighbors, in Harlem. He then toured with an evangelist's show, before joining the resident band at Minton's. In 1941 he made his first record, accompanying guitarist Charlie Christian, and went on to record with Art Blakey for Blue Note. During the forties and fifties, Monk and his protégé, Bud Powell, developed a piano style that perfectly matched the approach of bebop horn players such as Charlie Parker and Dizzy Gillespie.

However, the early fifties were a lean time for Monk, partly because his music was ahead of its time, and partly because a drug conviction made it difficult for him to get work. During the latter part of the decade his career picked up, and he recorded such albums as *Brilliant Corners*—with Sonny Rollins and Max Roach, displaying his humor with sophisticated, witty songs such as "I Surrender Dear"—*Thelonious Himself,* and *Thelonious Monk with John Coltrane*. All three albums are now regarded as masterpieces. By the sixties, Monk, once even the subject of the cover story in *Time* magazine, was acknowledged as one of the architects of modern jazz. In the early seventies, he worked with Dizzy Gillespie, Sonny Stitt, and Art Blakey in the band the Giants of Jazz with great success. But shortly afterward he retired from public view and lived quietly in Weehawken, New Jersey, until his death.

Although Thelonious Monk is now regarded as a formative influence on modern jazz, he spent many years being misunderstood as a performer and little known as an artist.

JELLY ROLL MORTON

1 8 9 0 — 1 9 4 1

JELLY ROLL MORTON was the first great jazz composer. He was a flamboyant character who began his career in the early 1900s as a pianist in the brothels of Storyville in New Orleans, and hustled a living at various points in his life as a pimp, gambler, and boxing promoter. Morton claimed to have invented jazz. Such boasts attracted the scorn of his contemporary Duke Ellington, who considered him vulgar, and have also tended to obscure his very real achievements as a musical innovator. Morton was undoubtedly the first jazz musician to blend ragtime, Creole, and Spanish habañera with mainstream thirties' jazz, creating arrangements that featured swinging background riffs and solo instrumental breaks. These were the key elements of the big-band sound, and many of Morton's compositions such as "King Porter Stomp" and "Jelly Roll Blues" later became jazz standards.

Morton was born Ferdinand La Menthe in New Orleans and learned piano as a child, absorbing the rich traditions of black music in the city. As a young man, he traveled around the U.S. in vaudeville shows, and also led his own bands in Chicago and Vancouver. In the twenties and based in Chicago, he made a series of classic recordings, including "King Porter Stomp," "Mr. Jelly Lord," and "Tom Cat Blues," as well as duetting with King Oliver. He went on to play and record with his band, the seven- or eight-piece Red Hot Peppers, adding his singing to tracks such as "Shoe Shine Drag" and "Mournful Serenade." He had a number of national hits during the twenties, such as "Black Bottom Stomp" and "Wolverine Blues," but by the early thirties, his style of playing with a small group was considered old-fashioned.

Although the big bands of the era continued to play his songs, and some of them, such as "Milenberg Joys" and "King Porter Stomp," became influential pieces in the new swing era, it was not until 1939 that he recorded again, in a group featuring Sidney Bechet. These recordings, made for the Library of Congress at the request of folklorist Alan Lomax, included recollections from his early days and revealed Morton as one of the earliest musician/historians. They also heralded renewed interest in his music. Soon after that, however, ill health prevented him from continuing his career, and he died in 1941.

Although Morton's claim to have invented jazz was questioned in some quarters, there is no doubt that he was the first important jazz composer and an innovative ensemble arranger.

MUDDY WATERS

1 9 1 5 — 1 9 8 3

MUDDY WATERS PERSONIFIES the Chicago blues sound. He grew up in the cotton fields of Mississippi, getting his nickname as a young boy when he liked playing in a muddy creek. Later he moved to Chicago where he broke away from country blues and began to play electric guitar over a heavy dance rhythm, developing what came to be known as urban blues. Urban blues from Chicago later became the major component of R&B, and, indirectly, of soul music. Waters himself went on to become a hero in the sixties' folk revival, and was the single most important influence on British beat groups such as the Rolling Stones, who named themselves after his hit of 1950. Through groups such as the Stones, Waters, along with other blues artists such as Willie Dixon, became known to a new generation of white music fans throughout America and Europe. Although many of the British groups copied his style, on the whole they gave him credit for it; as Waters once said, "They stole my music, but they gave me my name."

McKinley Morganfield, a.k.a. Muddy Waters, was born in Rolling Fork, Mississippi. He taught himself to play harmonica as a child, and later picked up guitar by listening to bluesmen such as Son House and Robert Johnson. In 1941 he was recorded by folklorist Alan Lomax for the Library of Congress. In 1943 he moved to Chicago, playing the South Side clubs there, along with Sonny Boy Williamson and Big Bill Broonzy. In the late forties and early fifties, he toured regularly with the Muddy Waters Blues Band. By then playing an electric guitar, Waters grew into a fine player and a singer of great intensity. He had several R&B hits on the Chess label, including "I Can't Be Satisfied," "Hoochie Coochie Man," "Rollin' Stone," and "Mannish Boy."

During the fifties, Waters and his band, which included harmonica player Little Walter and pianist Otis Spann, became hugely influential in black music, creating a repertoire of classic songs such as "Got My Mojo Working," collected on the 1959 album *The Best of Muddy Waters*, his first album release. Throughout the sixties, he played at major folk and jazz festivals, inspiring a whole new generation of young white musicians both in America and Europe; in the seventies, he went on to play with acolytes such as Michael Bloomfield, Paul Butterfield, Georgie Fame, Steve Winwood, and Johnny Winter. This last collaboration was very successful and resulted in two fine albums, *Hard Again* in 1977 and *I'm Ready* a year later, showing Waters at his best.

A fine live performer, Waters gave a legendary performance at the 1960 Newport Folk Festival.

YOUSSOU N'DOUR

b . 1 9 5 9

Youssou N'Dour is one of a long line of pioneers of a modern style of African pop, fusing traditional elements of his Senegalese musical culture with American and European influences. He represents a generation of African musicians who grew up thoroughly steeped in the rock music of the West, listening to artists such as Jimi Hendrix, and who went on to use their own rich African musical vocabulary to make a comparable style of contemporary music. Along with artists such as Baaba Maal, Salif Keïta, and Angelique Kidjo, N'Dour is one of a new breed of international African pop stars, whose music contains such a variety of cultural elements that it can truly be said to be global.

N'Dour was born in Dakar, Senegal, and grew up in the tough Medina section of the city. He is a hereditary *griot*—*griots* are musicians believed to have originated as Islamic hymnists who served West Africa's Mandingo kings. As a child, N'Dour sang at neighborhood parties in the area and, by the age of twelve, he was performing regularly on stage. In his teens he sang with the Star Band, Senegal's most popular group at that time. In 1979 he formed the Etoile De Dakar, which two years later became the Super Etoile. The Super Etoile went on to become the most successful band in Africa.

In 1986 he was invited to tour with British singer-songwriter Peter Gabriel, thus introducing him to audiences around the world. Gabriel's 1986 album *So* featured contributions from N'Dour, exposing him to an even wider audience. He subsequently headlined on Amnesty International's human rights tour, meeting jazz saxophonist Branford Marsalis, with whom he later collaborated. In 1989 he released his album *The Lion*, followed a year later by *Set*. Both albums brought him great acclaim, and critics compared him in stature to Bob Marley, hailing him as the newest star to emerge from the Third World. Since then N'Dour has produced his own albums at his Xippi studio in Dakar—including *Eyes Open* and *The Guide*, which yielded the hit single "7 Seconds" with Neneh Cherry.

By arranging ancient West African melodies for electric instruments, Youssou N'Dour has succeeded in melding traditional musical influences with those of the Caribbean and U.S. His unique blend of music has proved to be enormously popular both with European and American festivals and dance DJs. He is pictured here in performance in 1988.

NOTORIOUS B.I.G.

1973 – 1997

THE NOTORIOUS B.I.G., also known as Biggie Smalls, shot to fame with his 1994 debut album *Ready to Die*. The record went platinum, and Notorious B.I.G. was named rapper of the year at the 1995 Billboard Awards. The album painted a striking picture of life in the ghetto, as B.I.G. told stories of his former life as a crack dealer on the streets of New York and his rags-to-riches rise to fame. B.I.G.'s style of delivery was also extremely powerful: a huge man weighing 280 pounds (127 kg), his voice was deep and resonant.

Ready to Die immediately made him a star, yet he did not completely abandon his former life, and was arrested by the police on several occasions for drug-running, carrying weapons, and violent behavior. In 1997 he was preparing advance publicity for his second album, *Life After Death…Til Death Do Us Part*, when he was shot dead in a drive-by shooting in Los Angeles. He was twenty-four, and the father of two young children. There were many theories about why he was killed and about who killed him, but to date no one has been charged with the murder.

B.I.G.'s real name was Christopher Wallace. He grew up in the tough project buildings of Bedford-Stuyvesant, in Brooklyn, New York, the son of a preschool teacher. As a young man, he began to make a living selling crack, but was caught and imprisoned for nine months.

On his release, he made some demo tapes that impressed Uptown Records' boss André Harrell and producer Sean "Puffy" Combs, also known as Puff Daddy. Harrell signed Wallace, and over the next few years the Notorious B.I.G., as he was then known, came to represent the East Coast rap scene, carrying on a very public feud with West Coast rappers—some believe that B.I.G.'s murder was in retaliation for the earlier killing of fellow rapper Tupac Shakur.

Whatever the truth, his life, his work, and his death have made him a hero to a new generation of disenchanted and disenfranchised young Americans. A week after B.I.G.'s funeral, the double CD *Life After Death* hit the top of the charts and stayed there for three weeks.

Until his death, Notorious B.I.G. was one of the super-rappers. His lyrics differed from those of other gangsta rappers in their matter-of-fact delivery and unique perspective as he sought to tell the truth about life on the street.

CHARLIE PARKER

1 9 2 0 — 1 9 5 5

THE GENIUS OF CHARLIE PARKER as an instrumentalist and musical revolutionary is recognized universally. "Bird" or "Yardbird," as he was nicknamed, was able to improvise melodies with extraordinary fluidity, releasing torrents of notes in quick succession but always retaining a deep blues feel to his music. The beauty and originality of his playing made him the most renowned soloist of his day, and he influenced all later jazz musicians.

During the forties—along with Dizzy Gillespie, Thelonious Monk, and Kenny Clarke—Parker pioneered modern jazz, creating bebop from the mainstream swing style of the era. However, Parker did not enjoy the fruits of his success for long. As a heroin addict and heavy drinker, his personal life was chaotic, and he had several periods of mental instability. In 1954 his daughter died while he was away on tour and, according to his friends and colleagues, he never recovered from this tragedy. Parker died the following year of drug and alcohol abuse. The doctor who issued his death certificate estimated his age at between fifty and sixty, yet in fact he was only thirty-four.

Parker grew up in Kansas City, the son of a small-time vaudeville entertainer. He played baritone saxophone in his school band before leaving at fifteen to play alto sax in local bands. He practiced incessantly, particularly refining his ability to move from one key to another. In 1940 he joined Jay McShann's orchestra and visited New York, where he met Thelonious Monk. He then played in the Earl Hines band, which included the young Dizzy Gillespie.

In 1945 Parker began to record under his own name, leading a group that included Miles Davis. Tracks such as "Koko" and "Billie's Bounce" heralded the arrival of bebop, and Parker followed up with a series of classic compositions such as "Ornithology," "A Night in Tunisia," and "Relaxing at Camarillo," a tune that recalled his six-month sojourn there as a mental patient.

Parker went on to collaborate with some of the best musicians of the day, including Bud Powell and Charles Mingus. However, toward the end of his life, his performances became erratic, causing one musician at the time to comment sadly, "He's just an historical figure now."

Parker (center) plays at the opening of the new Birdland restaurant in December 1949 with "Hot Lips" Page on trumpet and Lennie Tristano on piano.

WILSON PICKETT

b . 1 9 4 1

THE "WICKED PICKETT" was a handsome, immaculately dressed young singer who emerged from gospel music to become one of the biggest soul stars of the sixties. His greatest hit, as befitted his image as a ladykiller, was "In the Midnight Hour," co-written with Steve Cropper, guitarist with Booker T and the MGs. The song, featuring Pickett's raucous description of his lovemaking skills set against Cropper's trenchant guitar riffs, was produced by Jerry Wexler of Atlantic, and immediately became a soul classic when it was released in 1965. During the sixties, Pickett went on to score more hits in the same vein, including "Mustang Sally" and "I'm a Midnight Mover." His success in the pop charts continued in the seventies with hits produced by the architects of the Philadelphia sound, Kenny Gamble and Leon Huff.

Pickett was born in Prattville, Alabama, later moving with his family to Detroit. There he joined a vocal group called the Violinaires and sang in churches. He was soon recruited by a local R&B group, the Falcons, to sing lead. He adopted a singing style that was similar to that of the Reverend Julius Cheeks of the Sensational Nightingales, and the group had a major hit on the black charts with "I Found A Love."

ABOVE: *Pickett is best known for the hits he recorded in the sixties, including "Land of a Thousand Dances," "Mustang Sally," and "Funky Broadway."*

This success encouraged Pickett to launch a solo career, and in 1963 he released his first U.S. hit, "If You Need Me," later a bigger success for Solomon Burke. Pickett then signed to Atlantic, where producer Bert Berns cast him as a romantic crooner on a song called "Come Home Baby." The track failed to make an impact, and producer Jerry Wexler stepped in to help. He took Pickett to the Stax studios in Memphis, where Pickett cut all the classic sixties hits that today ensure his place in the history of black music.

OPPOSITE PAGE: *Pickett is here captured on film in Ghana by the makers of* Soul to Soul *as well as by members of the local press.*

BUD POWELL

1 9 2 4 – 1 9 6 6

COMPOSER AND PIANIST Bud Powell was one of the founders of modern jazz. His approach to the music was adventurous, and he played with many of the great jazz musicians of the day, notably Charlie Parker, Max Roach, and Charles Mingus. However, his life was characterized by a series of mental breakdowns, and in later years, his playing was adversely affected by heavy use of drugs, both prescribed and illegal, as well as alcohol. His painful final years inspired the 1986 film *Round Midnight*, in which his contemporary Dexter Gordon played the leading role.

Born Earl Powell in New York, Bud was the son of stride pianist William Powell. He began to play the piano at age six and studied classical music until he was fifteen, when he took up jazz. Encouraged by Thelonious Monk, he joined trumpeter Cootie Williams's swing band. He created an individual style that was characterized by long, exciting melodic runs punctuated by unevenly spaced chords. Powell's dynamic playing and exciting compositions quickly made him one of the central figures in the emerging bebop movement centered around Minton's jazz club in New York.

From 1942 Powell began recording with a variety of musicians for companies such as Blue Note and Verve. As a composer, his most fruitful years came in the early fifties with pieces such as "Hallucinations," "Dance of the Infidels," "Tempus Fugue-it," and "The Glass Enclosure."

His most memorable partnership was with Charlie Parker. Their performance in 1953 with Max Roach, Charles Mingus, and Dizzy Gillespie was recorded and released as *Quintet of the Year* on Verve. He also worked with musicians such as Fats Navarro, Kenny Clarke, and Sonny Rollins.

By 1955 Powell's personal problems were apparent and, at a gig with Charlie Parker and Charles Mingus, he was too drunk to play. Parker also appeared to be in a peculiar mental state and the two men quarreled, with Powell leaving the stage. In 1959 Powell moved to Paris, where he led a trio with Kenny Clark and enjoyed success across the country. He also recorded with Coleman Hawkins and Dexter Gordon. He returned to New York in 1964 and died there in 1966.

Bud Powell is pictured here in performance at the Blue Note in Paris in 1960. He became celebrated among jazz enthusiasts in France during the early sixties. A technically brilliant pianist, he remains one of jazz music's great innovators.

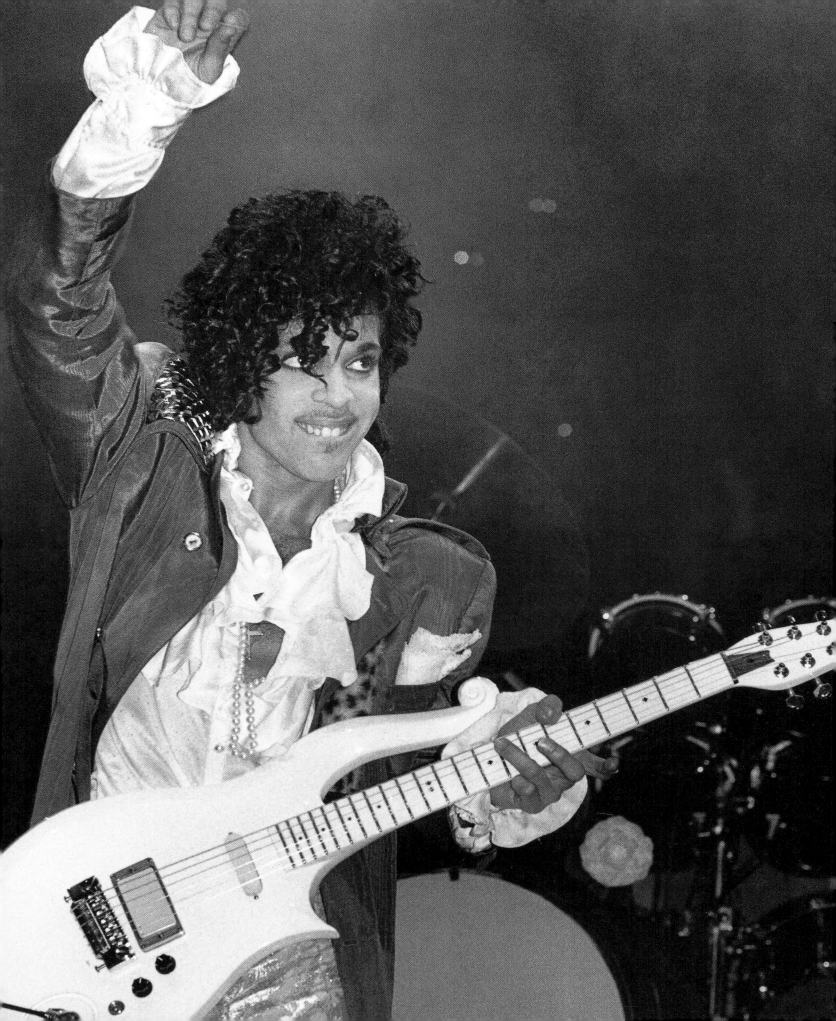

PRINCE

b . 1 9 5 8

IN THE EIGHTIES, Prince broke down the barriers between white rock music and black dance music, creating a sound that drew from many different sources—from funk and jazz to heavy metal. At his peak, his work was both highly innovative and strongly dance-oriented, an unusual combination in popular music.

His early songs were mainly concerned with sex—in the tradition of much funk and soul—yet their explicit lyrics were unconventional. In the same way, he presented an image of himself as highly sexual, in keeping with the pose of many black male singers, yet his sexuality was cryptic—for example, he would often wear women's underwear on stage. Black artists such as Little Richard in the fifties had mined this territory before, but what distinguished Prince was his ability to innovate musically over a wide range of styles for more than a decade.

Born in Minneapolis, Prince Rogers Nelson was named after his father's jazz group, the Prince Rogers Trio. By the time he was fifteen, he was able to play piano, guitar, and drums, and in 1972 he formed his first group, Champagne, while still in high school. Four years later, he moved to New York and was quickly signed by Warner Brothers, who recognized his prodigious talent. His first album, *For You*, was released in 1978; Prince played every instrument on the record. He followed up with *Prince, Dirty Mind,* and *Controversy,* an album that introduced political and social themes that were to reappear in later albums, such as *1999* and *Sign o' the Times.*

In 1984 Prince released *Purple Rain*, which was also a feature film. He went on to form a new backing group, the Revolution, making *Around the World in a Day* and *Parade*, which featured the hit single "Kiss." He then set up his own record company, Paisley Park, where he worked as a writer and producer for such artists as Sheila E. and Mavis Staples. In the late eighties, he continued to make successful albums, such as *Lovesexy* and the soundtrack to the hugely successful film *Batman*, but his popularity declined. He changed his name to a symbol and wanted to leave Warner Brothers, appearing in public with the word "slave" written on his face in reference to his contract with the label. Since then, with no name, no band, and no recording contract, he has released several albums on his own label, selling them through the Internet.

Prince sprang to superstar status with the release of his album Purple Rain *in 1984. He is shown here performing in New York in that year.*

PUBLIC ENEMY

CHUCK D (CARL RIDENHOUR) *b. 1965*   FLAVOR FLAV (WILL DRAYTON) *b. c.1962*

TERMINATOR X (NORMAN ROGERS) *b. c.1963*   PROFESSOR GRIFF (RICHARD GRIFFIN) *b. c.1965*

PUBLIC ENEMY WERE the first rap group to consciously ally themselves with the black radical tradition, drawing from both the Black Panther movement of the sixties and from their contemporaries in the eighties, the Nation of Islam. Their aim was to re-introduce politics onto the agenda of black music, drawing attention to the continued story of racial oppression in America and adopting a militant stance, expressed in raps such as "Don't Believe the Hype" and "Fight the Power."

Leader Chuck D, the son of New York political activists, was a skilled media manipulator, creating an image calculated to shock: the group wore army uniforms and their logo featured a black man caught in a gun sight. Yet Public Enemy touched on many serious issues confronting American society, bringing an angry intelligence to bear on subjects such as the criminalization of black people by state authorities and the failure of the black community to unite effectively against such treatment. They were also unique in being able to express black alienation and rage with real power, demanding that this be turned into political awareness and even action.

The group mounted several political campaigns, taking the governor of Arizona to task for refusing to honor Martin Luther King's birthday, and organizing a Black Awareness Program in education. They also helped break down racial barriers in music, performing a memorable gig with heavy metal group Anthrax at Madison Square Gardens in 1991.

However, Public Enemy's attempts to politicize young black people ultimately failed. Their shows often ended in violence and bad publicity, and a number of negative media reports put the group under the spotlight. They gradually lost their edge as West Coast gangsta rap became fashionable and hip-hop talk turned to gold, guns, and girls.

Formed in 1982, Public Enemy had a series of best-selling albums after signing with Def Jam and releasing *Yo! Bum Rush the Show* in 1987. Their two most important albums followed. In 1989 they released *It Takes a Nation of Millions to Hold Us Back,* and, in 1990, they released *Fear of a Black Planet*. They also collaborated with filmmaker Spike Lee, and were featured on the soundtracks of *Do the Right Thing* and *He Got Game*.

After the release of their critically acclaimed album It Takes a Nation of Millions to Hold Us Back, *Public Enemy toured Britain in 1990. They are pictured here in London.*

MA RAINEY

1 8 8 6 — 1 9 3 9

"THE MOTHER OF THE BLUES," Ma Rainey was the first of the great female blues singers. She influenced many other singers, including her contemporary Bessie Smith, and in the twenties her ability to write and sing songs with a unique Southern sensibility made her one of the top recording artists of the era.

She was born Gertrude Melissa Nix Pridgett in Columbus, Georgia. Her parents were entertainers, and from a young age, she worked in tent shows touring the southern states. In 1904 she married William Rainey, a minstrel comic, and formed a song and dance team with him. The pair of them appeared as Rainey and Rainey, or Ma and Pa Rainey, Assassinators of the Blues. When the partnership split up, Ma Rainey went on to perform on the vaudeville circuit in the South and Midwest, touring with the Rabbit's Foot Minstrels and others. She then formed her own troupe, which at one time included Bessie Smith.

ABOVE: *Ma Rainey and her Georgia Jazz Band performing in Chicago in 1923.*

During the twenties she recorded about a hundred songs for Paramount, singing with country blues and jazz musicians. She began with a backing band called the Lovie Austin Blue Serenaders, but later worked with a variety of musicians. Her best-known song is "See See Rider," on which she was accompanied by Louis Armstrong and pianist Fletcher Henderson. Other well-known songs are "Ma Rainey's Black Bottom," "Oh My Babe Blues," featuring saxophonist Coleman Hawkins, and "Deep Moanin' Blues," with guitarist Tampa Red.

Sadly, the Depression of the thirties brought a halt to Ma Rainey's career, both as a traveling entertainer and as a recording artist. She retired in 1933 and became the owner of two theaters in Georgia, also joining the Friendship Baptist Church.

OPPOSITE PAGE: *Ma Rainey is pictured here in 1923, the year she signed with Paramount. She sang with great power and feeling, and her songs incorporated references to folk culture.*

OTIS REDDING

1 9 4 1 – 1 9 6 7

OTIS REDDING WAS the most popular male soul singer of his time. He grew up in a gospel environment and developed an intense, impassioned style of delivery that could transform the most ordinary song into a deeply moving experience. He was also a songwriter of great talent, composing such beautiful ballads as "These Arms of Mine," which became his first hit, and "I've Been Loving You Too Long" (co-written with Jerry Butler). During the sixties, he became well known to audiences, first in Europe after touring there, and then in the U.S. after appearing at the Monterey Pop Festival in 1967. His career was tragically cut short when his private jet crashed into a lake outside Madison, Wisconsin, on December 10, 1967, killing him and four members of his band, the Bar-Kays.

From Dawson, Georgia, Otis Redding was the son of a minister. He began by singing in church, before performing in local clubs around his hometown. He then moved with his family to Macon, Georgia, where he joined an established band, Johnny Jenkins and the Pinetoppers. When the band were signed to Atlantic, they were given some studio time. At the end of one session, there was some time to spare, so Redding was allowed to use it to record his own composition, "These Arms of Mine." The single was released and became a Top 20 R&B hit in 1963. Redding then released his debut album, *Pain in My Heart*, which contained such classics as "That's How Strong My Love Is" and "Respect," later recorded by Aretha Franklin.

In 1965 Redding's version of "My Girl," written by Smokey Robinson, reached the U.K. charts, and the following year, he toured in Europe, establishing himself as a favorite among white audiences there and scoring a hit with his version of the Rolling Stones' "Satisfaction." In the U.S., he had hits with "Fa-Fa-Fa-Fa-Fa (Sad Song)," "Try a Little Tenderness," and a cover of Sam Cooke's "Shake." But it was the three albums released in 1966—*Otis Blue, The Soul Album,* and *The Dictionary of Soul*—that are now regarded as his finest work. He had just recorded his version of the Christmas song "Merry Christmas Baby," written by Charles Brown in 1947, and was at the peak of his success, when he met his death in 1967. A song he had written with Steve Cropper of Booker T and the MGs, "(Sittin' on) the Dock of the Bay," was released posthumously, and became a number one hit.

Redding's vocal range was huge: He could use power, he could croon, and he could testify.

SMOKEY ROBINSON

b. 1940

SMOKEY ROBINSON'S beautifully crafted songs once prompted Bob Dylan to call him America's greatest living poet. Smokey Robinson could take the most banal phrase and make something magical of it, creating elegant metaphors and narratives around a simple cliché. Most of his songs were pretty, romantic confections, yet his light touch showed a wit and intelligence often lacking in the pop genre. Robinson also had a lovely, high singing voice, which perfectly expressed his melodies and lyrics, and his good looks were said to have made girls faint, especially when he sang the "ooo" in his hit song of 1965, "Ooo Baby Baby." During the sixties, with his group the Miracles, Robinson performed classic songs such as "Tracks of My Tears" and "I Second That Emotion," while also writing and producing memorable hits for other top Motown acts such as Mary Wells, Marvin Gaye, the Temptations, and the Supremes.

Robinson came from Detroit, where he formed the Miracles while still in high school. When Berry Gordy set up Tamla Motown in 1958, he signed the Miracles, who went on to score the label's first hit, "Shop Around." The Miracles' next big success

was "You've Really Got a Hold on Me," which was later covered by the Beatles. Throughout the sixties, the Miracles went on to score numerous chart hits, and were still popular at the beginning of the next decade, when "The Tears of a Clown" reached the charts. At the same time, Robinson became one of Motown's foremost staff writers and producers, as well as helping Gordy to run the business side of the label.

During the seventies, Motown moved from Detroit to Los Angeles, and Robinson left the Miracles, gradually becoming more and more absorbed in the corporate world of the company. In 1973 he returned to the recording studio, this time as a solo act, and released several albums, including *A Quiet Storm*, which featured the hit, "Baby that's Backatcha." In 1981 he scored a million-selling hit with the title track from *Being With You*. His later albums are not rated as highly as his early work, but some of them contain songs that have all the class and style of his sixties' hits.

OPPOSITE PAGE: *Smokey and the Miracles performing on the* Sound of Motown *TV show in March 1965.*

LEFT: *The band on tour with other Motown artists in London in 1965.*

SONNY ROLLINS

b . 1 9 3 0

SONNY ROLLINS WAS one of the greatest tenor saxophone players to emerge in jazz. His skill as an improviser was unrivaled: his inventiveness was so impressive that it caused some critics to compare his work with Louis Armstrong's innovations in the twenties. Rollins had grown up in New York, listening to an older generation of jazzmen, including Coleman Hawkins, Charlie Parker, Thelonious Monk, and Bud Powell, all of whom he later played with. In the fifties, he recorded with drummer Max Roach and trumpeter Clifford Brown, developing an exciting, rhythmic style and composing several of his best-known tunes, including "Oleo" and "Airegin." He also recorded with Miles Davis and John Coltrane. His career has been characterized by lengthy breaks from playing, sometimes caused by ill health and sometimes by general dissatisfaction at the state of the jazz scene, but he has continued to return to music, both in the studio and in the concert hall.

Rollins took piano lessons from age nine, but soon gave them up and began to play saxophone instead. He recorded his first tune, "Audubon," in 1948, and went on to play with the leading lights of the jazz world in New York. In 1954 he made a solo album, *Moving Out*, and the following year, joined Max Roach and Clifford Brown to form his own quintet. This was a fertile period in which he developed his own improvisational style, and from then on he continued to lead his own groups. His albums from this period include *Tenor Madness*, recorded with John Coltrane, and *Freedom Suite*, inspired by the black Civil Rights movement.

But Rollins was not always satisfied, either with his own performances or with those of his band members, and the line-up of his musicians changed frequently as did the style of his musical output. In the sixties, while searching for a suitable style for his technique, he recorded the calypso "Don't Stop the Carnival" and most of the music on the soundtrack to the movie *Alfie*, before taking a two-year break from playing music. The seventies saw him continue to experiment, this time with soul, bop, and funk and rock fusions. In 1986 his Concerto for Saxophone and Orchestra was premièred in Japan.

Sonny Rollins in the streets of Soho in London. No stranger to playing in the open air, Rollins is said to have practiced on the pedestrian crosswalk of the Williamsburg Bridge in New York so as not to disturb the neighbors.

DIANA ROSS

b . 1 9 4 4

THE FIRST BLACK woman superstar, Diana Ross was one of the few solo singers to emerge from the girl groups of the sixties. Unlike most of her contemporaries, she was able to build a long, highly successful career in the music industry once the girl-group boom was over. Widely criticized during the seventies for her ruthless ambition—a quality that, in a man, might have been viewed more sympathetically—Ross was also admired by her fellow artists for her professionalism and commitment to her work. Her ability to spot trends, such as the dance-oriented pop of the early eighties, gave her career a longevity that was quite new for a female artist in black music. She became something of a role model for women, particularly black women, in the days before those qualities were considered generally acceptable in female artists. In many ways Ross's pathbreaking career prefigures that of Madonna, and is all the more extraordinary given her social origins in the projects of Detroit and her career beginnings in the nameless, faceless girl-group pop industry of the sixties.

Diana Ross was born in Detroit, and as a teenager, together with her friends Mary Wilson and Florence Ballard, formed the Primettes. They were signed, as the Supremes, to Berry Gordy's Motown label, and had a huge run of hits from 1964 to 1970, when Ross launched her solo career.

Her first hit was "Reach Out and Touch (Somebody's Hand)," followed by "Remember Me," and "Touch Me in the Morning." Gordy, who had groomed Ross for stardom since the early days, then secured her the role as Billie Holiday in *Lady Sings the Blues*, her most successful film part. Later screen roles, in *Mahogany* and *The Wiz*, were less well received. However, in 1980 Ross revived her musical career with *Diana*, a sparkling album produced by Nile Rodgers and Bernard Edwards of Chic, which yielded several big hits. After a massive hit duetting with Lionel Ritchie on "Endless Love," Ross left Motown and produced her own album, *Why Do Fools Fall in Love*. She went on to release several more albums, collaborating with artists such as Michael Jackson and Barry Gibb of the Bee Gees.

OPPOSITE PAGE: *Diana Ross: the first black woman superstar.*
RIGHT: *The Supremes on the* Sound of Motown *TV show in the mid-sixties.*

GIL SCOTT-HERON

b . 1 9 4 9

DURING THE SEVENTIES, poet and novelist Gil Scott-Heron became one of the most important dissenting political voices in black music. He commented on most of the burning issues of the day, such as apartheid ("Johannesburg"), the space race ("Whitey on the Moon"), political corruption ("H^{2}O-Gate"), political leaders ("B-Movie"—referring to President Reagan's former career as a Hollywood actor), and the media ("The Revolution Will Not Be Televised"). He also tackled some of the social problems besetting black people in America: for example, in "The Bottle," which discussed alcoholism, and in "Home Is Where the Hatred Is," about heroin addiction. His albums, which often featured half-spoken, half-sung verses, prefigured today's rap music, both in terms of their musical style and their political content.

Scott-Heron was born in Chicago, but was raised by his grandmother in Jackson, Tennessee. During his teens, he wrote detective stories, but after the death of his grandmother, he turned to politics. He moved to New York and studied literary composition before writing several novels, including *The Vulture* and *The Nigger Factory*. He then teamed up with keyboard player Brian Jackson to record a collection of his poems set to music. This was released as *Small Talk at 125th Street* and *Lenox* on the Flying Dutchman label in 1972. His subsequent albums on the label, *Free Will, Pieces of a Man*, and *The Revolution Will Not Be Televised*, earned him a large cult following.

In 1975 he signed to the Arista label, making such albums as *From South Africa to South Carolina*, which earned him an international reputation. In the late seventies, he recorded several classic and eloquent songs on the subject of nuclear power, such as "South Carolina (Barnwell)," "We Almost Lost Detroit," and "Shut 'Em Down." In 1980 he split with Jackson and formed a touring band, Amnesia Express. He went on to make a series of solo albums, including *Real Eyes, Reflections*, and *Moving Target*, each of which contained songs, such as "B-Movie" and "Re-Ron," which captured perfectly the mood of contemporary left-wing politics. In the nineties, Scott has continued to record and tour both as a poet and a singer. Despite his hectic schedule and reported problems with drugs, his material continues to be fresh, vibrant, topical, and bitterly opposed to the hypocrisy of politicians.

Gil Scott-Heron performing on stage in 1976. Scott-Heron often described Brian Jackson, his long-time collaborator, and himself as "interpreters of the black experience."

Tupac Shakur

1 9 7 1 — 1 9 9 6

THE SHORT, TUMULTUOUS LIFE of Tupac Shakur was reflected in a series of albums that made him, along with his rival, the Notorious B.I.G., one of the leading rappers of his generation. Like many of his peers, his raps were expressions of violence, rage, and frustration, and he was graphic in his descriptions of sexual conquests; at the same time, his work often contained lyrically expressed emotions and political reflections that marked him out from the crowd. He also developed a style of rapping that was unique, emphasizing the last parts of his phrases in a syncopated way. In addition to his talent as a rapper, Shakur was a charismatic, handsome man who seemed set to forge a successful career as an actor, gaining favorable reviews for his performances in several films, including *Bullet*, *Gang Related*, *Gridlock'd*, and *Rhyme and Reason*.

Born in the Bronx, New York City, and named after the last king of the Incas, Tupac Amaru, Shakur was the son of Afeni Shakur, a Black Panther political activist, and Billy Garland, a father who was largely absent while he was growing up. His home life was unstable, and he moved around constantly with his mother, often living in shelters but eventually settling in Baltimore. As a young man, he moved to California. He became involved in gang warfare and had constant run-ins with the law.

In 1992, as 2Pac, he released *2Pacalypse Now*, an album that documented his life as a gangster, and which became a major target for politician Dan Quayle's attempts to counter the bad influence of Hollywood in returning to traditional values. The following year, his next release, *Strictly 4 My N.I.G.G.A.Z.*, crossed over to the pop charts. Yet despite his success, Shakur continued to find himself in trouble, serving eight months in prison in 1994 on a conviction for sexual abuse. Shortly after his release, he miraculously survived five gunshot wounds when thieves made off with his jewelry. Shortly afterward he signed for Death Row Records and went on to make his finest albums, *Me Against the World* and *All Eyez On Me*, which sold over five million copies and gave him a number one hit single with "How Do You Want It." During this time, a rivalry had developed between the East Coast and the West Coast rap scenes—the so-called gangsta wars. Dark words were spoken by both sides after Shakur's shooting in 1994. In 1996 Shakur was killed in a drive-by shooting on Flamingo Road in Las Vegas. No one has been convicted of the murder.

A talented lyricist with a gift for storytelling, Shakur's potential was not fulfilled in his lifetime.

NINA SIMONE

b . 1 9 3 3

NINA SIMONE IS one of the great divas of black music. Her singing and playing is unclassifiable: She approaches blues, soul, pop, and folk songs in a unique, intensely emotional, personal style. Trained as a classical pianist, Simone made popular music recordings in the fifties, before becoming involved with the Civil Rights movement in the sixties. Her militant stance alienated the music industry and almost destroyed her career, but her integrity has earned her tremendous respect all over the world, especially in Europe where she still has a loyal following.

Simone was born Eunice Waymon in Tryon, North Carolina, one of eight children who were all musical. Her parents were both Methodist ministers and she was raised in the gospel tradition. As a young woman, she attended the Juilliard School of Music in New York, but found that racism prevented her from pursuing a career as a classical pianist, and instead turned to pop. Her first major hit in the fifties was the song "I Loves You Porgy" from Gershwin's musical *Porgy and Bess*. During the sixties, she went on to have hits with covers of the Bee Gees' "To Love Somebody" and "Ain't Got No—I Got Life" from the musical *Hair*, as well as her own own composition, "To Be Young, Gifted, and Black."

Yet Simone was far more than a sixties pop singer. She became an icon of the Civil Rights movement, playing at benefits and writing songs such as "Mississippi Goddam" about the oppression of blacks in the South. She was friendly with the poet Langston Hughes and other well-known radical figures, and adopted a high-profile political role, speaking out against injustice and racial discrimination. With the end of the Civil Rights movement, Simone's career faltered, her marriage failed, and her home was confiscated by the authorities on tax charges. She traveled to Africa and then to France, where she played small nightclubs to earn a living.

During the seventies, she recorded the albums *It Is Finished* and *Baltimore*, the title track of which was a beautiful rendition of the Randy Newman song. In the eighties, she had an unexpected hit with "My Baby Just Cares for Me," an obscure recording she had made in the fifties that was picked up and used in a TV commercial for Chanel perfume. Sadly, she received very few royalties for the record.

During her first public recital, Simone saw her parents removed from the hall to make room for whites. This probably reinforced her commitment to the fight for racial equality.

BESSIE SMITH

1 8 9 4 — 1 9 3 7

KNOWN AS THE "Empress of the Blues," Bessie Smith is regarded as the greatest woman blues singer of all time. Her singing has a dignity, intensity, and depth of feeling that successors such as Billie Holiday and Dinah Washington used as a model in creating their own vocal styles. Smith's subtle phrasing and intonation also influenced many jazz instrumentalists. But for many, Smith was more than just a blues singer. At a time when neither black performers nor women were tolerated in the white-dominated entertainment industry, Smith's forceful personality, legendary lifestyle, and success made her a legend and gave hope to the oppressed.

Born in Chattanooga, Tennessee, and one of seven children, Bessie Smith was orphaned at age seven and sang in the streets to earn money. By age twelve she was touring with blues singer Ma Rainey. In 1915 Smith toured with the Rabbit's Foot Minstrels, and went on to perform in vaudeville in Atlantic City and Philadelphia. By age twenty-four she was starring in her own review, *Liberty Belles.*

In 1923 Smith began a recording career with Columbia Records, and had her first hit with "Down-Hearted Blues." The following year, she initiated Columbia's new "race" catalog—records targeted specifically at a black audience—with "Chicago-Bound Blues." Later that same year, she made a record with Louis Armstrong, "The St. Louis Blues," which went on to become one of her best-known songs.

Smith was accompanied by some of the best blues and jazz musicians of the time, including Clarence Williams, Fletcher Henderson, James P. Johnson, Coleman Hawkins, Buster Bailey, Charlie Green, and Benny Goodman. She also performed two duets, "Far Away Blues" and "I'm Going Back to My Used to Be," with another blues singer of the time, Clara Smith, who was known as the "Queen of the Moaners."

During the twenties, Smith was a star attraction at black music halls all over the U.S., often mounting her own shows such as *Harlem Frolics* and *Happy Days.* However, by the thirties, vaudeville was beginning to be seen as old-fashioned, and this, together with the Depression, caused her career to decline. In 1931 she was dropped by Columbia, and returned to touring in small shows. Producer John Hammond tried to revive her career, recording her in an up-tempo "swing" style, but her heyday was over. In 1937 she died after an auto accident in Clarksdale, Mississippi, while on tour.

More than just one of the best blues singer of all time, Smith's success gave hope to the oppressed.

THE STAPLE SINGERS

ROEBUCK POPS STAPLES *b.* *1915* CLEOTHA STAPLES *b.* *1934*
MAVIS STAPLES *b.* *1940* PERVIS STAPLES *b.* *1935*
YVONNE STAPLES *b.* *1939*

POPS STAPLES AND his children Cleo, Mavis, Pervis, and Yvonne were one of America's greatest gospel groups. They found success in the pop market with a series of message songs that chimed with the relaxed, positive mood among black people that still prevailed in the years following the Civil Rights movement. Their early gospel recordings in the fifties included "Amazing Grace," "Stand By Me," and "This May Be the Last Time," which later became pop hits for other artists. In the sixties, the Staple Singers moved toward folk-gospel, and by the seventies, they were singing secular songs with a strong message of hope, faith, and love that struck a chord with many pop fans—songs such as "Respect Yourself," "I'll Take You There," and "If You're Ready (Come Go With Me)." The group's gospel roots gave their secular songs a warmth, compassion, and genuine sense of optimism rarely achieved in pop music, and in Mavis Staples the group had a wonderful singer of intense emotional depth.

Roebuck Pops Staples grew up in Winona, Mississippi, and played blues guitar under the influence of Delta bluesmen such as Robert Johnson. At age fifteen, he saw the light and entered the church. He toured with the Golden Trumpets before settling in Chicago with his wife, Oceola, in 1936. He continued to play music while working in a steel mill to support his growing family, and in 1951 formed a group with his daughters and son who had all inherited his musical talent. They recorded their debut single, "Sit Down Servant," and went on to sign with the Vee-Jay label, releasing a series of gospel successes, beginning with "Uncloudy Day" in 1955. During the sixties, the group signed to Stax, where Al Bell produced their run of hits, beginning in 1971 with "Respect Yourself." In 1976 they signed to Curtis Mayfield's Curtom label, and soon afterward they had a number one hit with the theme song to a Sidney Poitier/Bill Cosby movie called *Let's Do It Again*.

In the eighties and nineties, both Pops and Mavis concentrated on solo projects, and with some success. Mavis signed to Prince's Paisley Park label, to the consternation of many of her gospel fans, while Pops recorded and released the album *Peace to the Neighborhood* in 1992.

The Staple Singers' live performances were inspirational and were captured in two films released in the 1970s, Wattstax *and* Soul to Soul, *from which this still was taken.*

SLY STONE

b. 1 9 4 4

SLY AND THE FAMILY STONE were one of the first black groups to wholeheartedly embrace the sixties counterculture, playing music that celebrated the hedonism of the hippie lifestyle yet also introduced serious political issues into it. During the late sixties and seventies, the group became popular worldwide, scoring hits such as "Dance to the Music," "Everyday People," "Thank You (Falletin Me Be Mice Elf Agin)," and "Family Affair." They also released protest songs about racial prejudice in society, such as "Don't Call Me Nigger, Whitey," inspiring other black acts such as the Temptations to follow suit. However, Sly Stone's career was soon cut short by his problems with drug dependency: he often failed to show up at gigs, and his musical output became erratic. During the seventies, a whole generation of black musicians showed themselves to be deeply influenced by Stone, among them George Clinton, Rick James, Prince, and Michael Jackson.

Sly Stone was born Sylvester Stewart in Dallas, Texas, and made his recording debut at age four, singing a gospel song, "On the Battlefield for My Lord." After singing with a group called the Viscannes in high school, he moved to San Francisco, where he became a disc jockey. He then went into record production before forming his own group, the Stoners, with his sister Rose, brother Freddie, and cousin Larry Graham. The group were signed to CBS and changed their name to Sly and the Family Stone. Their 1968 album *Dance to the Music* was an innovative blend of rock and soul,

which ignored the barriers between black and white music, combining an R&B beat and jazz-styled horns with psychedelic guitars and socially conscious lyrics. The album was followed by *Life*, *Stand!*, *There's a Riot Going On*, and *Fresh*, after which their albums sales began to decline.

OPPOSITE PAGE: *Stone performing in the seventies.* RIGHT: *Stone was one of the first people to include black and white men and women in his band. (From left to right): Sly, Larry Graham, Rose, Cynthia Robinson, Freddie, Greg Errico, and Jerry Martini.*

SUN RA

1 9 1 4 — 1 9 9 3

"I'M ACTUALLY PAINTING pictures of infinity with my music, and that's why a lot of people can't understand it." So said Sun Ra, leader of the earliest experimental black big band, the Solar Arkestra, otherwise known as the Band from Outer Space. Sun Ra was a kind of maverick Duke Ellington. He led his band for over thirty years, earning the respect and loyalty of great musicians such as trombonist Julian Priester and saxophonist John Gilmore, who many regard as the mentor of John Coltrane. The Arkestra's concerts were a bizarre spectacle, conjuring up images both of ancient Egypt and of futuristic space-age civilizations: Musicians clothed in flowing robes wore helmets with lights flashing on their heads and ran about the stage chasing each other while playing, often breaking into chants of "Space is the place." Yet for all the band's zany theatricality, it was actually a highly disciplined, professional group of musicians run with great authority by its leader. Always an innovator, Sun Ra has consistently used new keyboard instruments to explore new sounds.

Sun Ra was born on the planet Saturn, but made his earthly appearance in Birmingham, Alabama, under the name of Herman Sonny Blount. He took piano lessons as a child, studying under noted pianist Fess Wheatley. As a young man, he attended Alabama Agricultural and Mechanical College but dropped out and moved to Chicago to become a jazz musician. During the forties, he learned his craft scoring music for nightclub shows in Chicago, and worked with the great swing bandleader Fletcher Henderson. In the fifties, he formed the Arkestra, encouraging his musicians to play free, using modal scales and synthesizers, well before anyone else in jazz. The Arkestra moved to New York in the sixties, recording albums such as *The Magic City* and *The Heliocentric Worlds of Sun Ra*. In the seventies, Sun Ra began to reach a bigger audience. The Arkestra toured American colleges and universities, and often performed in Europe, where they gained a cult following. In 1976 they even appeared on prime-time American TV on *Saturday Night Live*.

The Arkestra was so far ahead of their time that, in the eighties, they continued to be seen as innovative. With their live shows combining multimedia elements, the slide and light shows, modern dance, and new-age astronomical and Egyptian imagery, Sun Ra and the Arkestra can even be said to have presaged the nineties.

Sun Ra and the Arkestra performing in New York's Central Park in 1987.

THE TEMPTATIONS

MELVIN FRANKLIN *1942–1995* EDDIE KENDRICKS *1939–1991*
ELDRIDGE BRYANT *b. 1941, replaced by* DAVID RUFFIN *1941–1990,*
then by DENNIS EDWARDS *b. 1943* OTIS WILLIAMS *b. 1941*
PAUL WILLIAMS *1939–1973*

THE TEMPTATIONS WERE the ultimate expression of Berry Gordy's vision for Motown: a top-quality act with great songs, fine singing, and the slickest dance routines in town. The group became a vehicle for successive waves of Motown songwriters, from Smokey Robinson, who provided them with their early hits in the sixties, to Norman Whitfield, who wrote and produced their later successes. Between 1964 and 1975, the Temptations scored over twenty major chart hits, ranging from tender, romantic ballads to scorching songs of social protest.

The group began their career as the Elgins and changed their name to the Primes; their sister group was the Primettes, who later became the Supremes. When Berry Gordy signed them to Motown, they became the Temptations. Gordy assigned Smokey Robinson to write and produce them, and in 1964 "The Way You Do the Things You Do" reached the Top 20. The following year, "My Girl" topped the charts, a beautiful love song with all the hallmarks of a Robinson masterpiece. But despite more great releases, the group did not achieve another number one, so in 1966 Norman Whitfield took over. He worked with songwriters Brian Holland and Barrett Strong, writing songs such as "Cloud Nine," "Psychedelic Shack," and "Ball of Confusion" that reflected the turbulence of the times and made reference to psychedelic music with wailing electric guitars. At the same time, the group proved themselves capable of handling anything: from the plaintive beauty of "Just My Imagination" and "I Can't Get Next to You" to the funk of "Papa Was a Rolling Stone."

From 1968, when David Ruffin left the group to be replaced by Dennis Edwards, there were numerous line-up changes: Eddie Kendricks was replaced by Damon Harris, and Paul Williams by Richard Street. Things were not going well for the group, particularly with the suicide of Paul Williams in 1973. Yet the Temptations, with their unique sound, exquisite harmonies, and classy stage act, continued to thrive as live performers until well into the eighties.

By 1973, when this photograph was taken, Otis Williams (second from left) was the only member of the original line-up. The others shown here are (from left): Dennis Edwards, Damon Harris, David English, and Richard Street.

SISTER ROSETTA THARPE

1 9 1 5 — 1 9 7 3

SISTER ROSETTA THARPE was a tremendously influential gospel singer who drew on both church music and the blues to create a lively, urban sound that brought her many secular admirers. Her trenchant guitar style was an early model for the rock'n'roll riffs of Chuck Berry and others. Unlike her contemporary, Mahalia Jackson, Tharpe often sang with blues musicians, blurring the line between entertainment and worship. Her high-spirited, exuberant approach to gospel struck a chord with jazz and pop fans. After her recording heyday in the forties, she went on to tour Europe and America during the fifties and sixties, to great acclaim.

She was born Rosetta Nubin in Cotton Plant, Arkansas, the daughter of Katie Bell Nubin, a traveling gospel shouter and pianist. Rosetta was raised in Chicago as a member of the Holiness Church. There she learned how to sing and play acoustic guitar, later switching to electric guitar. She was influenced by the gospel of her church, but was also attracted to the blues music of Arkansas and the jazz she heard in Chicago. In 1934 she married pastor Wilbur Thorpe, changed her name to Tharpe, and moved to New York. Her first professional engagement was as a singer with Cab Calloway's Revue, and she later went on to sing with Lucky Millinder and his band. She recorded songs such as "Pickin' the Cabbage," "I Want a Tall, Skinny Papa," and "Shout Sister Shout." On some recordings, such as "That's All," she showed off a rocking guitar style that was years ahead of its time. She also pursued a solo career as a cabaret artist, appearing at sophisticated venues such as Café Society in New York City.

From the mid-forties, Tharpe reverted to her gospel roots, recording only religious songs. She cut a number of songs for Decca—some of them duets with her mother, Kate, and some with Sister Marie Knight—that have become classics of the genre, including "Didn't It Rain" and "Up Above My Head." In 1953 Tharpe married Russell Morrison, a former manager of the Ink Spots, who took charge of her career. Tharpe continued to record and perform live, mostly at jazz festivals, until the seventies, once touring Europe on crutches after her leg was amputated following a stroke. She died on the first scheduled day of recording for a new album.

Sister Rosetta Tharpe played music that mixed gospel, blues, and jazz. She was a good singer with a gruff, smoky voice, but it was the brilliance of her guitar playing that made her stand out from the crowd. Here she is performing with Chris Barber's Jazz Band in 1957.

BIG MAMA THORNTON

1 9 2 6 — 1 9 8 4

BIG MAMA THORNTON was a legendary blues singer who had a number one hit on the R&B charts with "Hound Dog" in 1953. The song, written by Jerry Leiber and Mike Stoller, was later covered by Elvis Presley. Although Thornton did not actually write the song, some critics felt that her interpretation of it was so strong that it warranted a credit on Elvis's disc. A powerful singer in the tradition of Ma Rainey, Bessie Smith, and Memphis Minnie, Big Mama Thornton toured the American South in the forties, working in vaudeville, before singing with bands in the fifties. During the sixties, along with contemporaries such as Howlin' Wolf and Muddy Waters, she toured the U.S. and Europe, playing at folk and jazz festivals as well as at black clubs and bringing her music to a new generation of young fans.

Willie Mae Thornton was born in Montgomery, Alabama, the daughter of a minister. She taught herself to play harmonica and drums, and as a young woman, joined Sammy Green's Georgia-based Hot Harlem Revue, for whom she sang, danced, and told jokes—for seven years. She later went on to tour with bandleader Johnny Otis's Rhythm and Blues Caravan, with whom she recorded her version of "Hound Dog." The record was a hit and brought her fame, but no fortune. She went on to work with blues singer and harmonica player Little Junior Parker and bandleader Clarence "Gatemouth" Brown. Her star began to wane in the late fifties, so she moved to San Francisco to revive her career playing in local clubs around the Bay area. She also sang with Roy Milton's band in Los Angeles in a popular jump-blues style. Thornton was such a versatile singer that she could adapt to any style, from downhome acoustic blues to electric urban soul.

During the sixties, Big Mama Thornton toured Europe with the American Folk Blues Festival, recording her first album, *Big Mama Thornton in Europe*, for the Arhoolie label, along with fellow performers such as Mississippi Fred McDowell and Buddy Guy. In 1969 she released *Stronger Than Dirt*, an album that featured her composition "Ball and Chain," later covered by Janis Joplin. In the seventies, she released *Jail*, an album of her performances in prisons, and also recorded with zydeco star Clifton Chenier before retiring from the business.

Big Mama Thornton warms up with her harmonica backstage at the 4th American Folk Blues Festival at the Fairfields Hall in Croydon, England, in 1965.

TINA TURNER

b .   1 9 3 8

TINA TURNER is an icon of black music today, not only because of her talent as a singer, but also because she is seen to have triumphed in the face of adversity, liberating herself from an oppressive marriage to become one of rock's major stars. During the sixties, she sang in her husband Ike Turner's R&B band, also recording "River Deep Mountain High" with pop producer Phil Spector. In the seventies, Ike and Tina's careers continued to flourish with hits such as "Proud Mary" and "Nutbush City Limits," but she became increasingly unhappy in her marriage as her husband became more and more violent and controlling toward her. In 1976 she left him, and without his financial and musical support, looked set to pursue a career on the oldies circuit, recycling her former hits along with other sixties stars. However, she managed to fight her way back into the pop charts with a version of Al Green's "Let's Stay Together," and from then on, her career took off.

During the eighties, she had several hit albums and toured constantly, performing in massive stadiums around the world. Her success was extraordinary: not only was she one of the first black women to become a superstar within the white rock mainstream, but she also continued to present an energetic, sexual image on stage until well into her fifties.

Turner was born Annie Mae Bullock in Brownsville, Tennessee, and first met Ike Turner in a St. Louis nightclub when she got up to sing with his band. He added her to the line-up, and the pair were later married. The band toured as the Ike and Tina Turner Revue during the sixties and seventies, recording a number of hits that some critics now regard as her best work. Tina then launched a solo career that took a while to get going. In 1983 she worked with members of the group Heaven 17 on a cover version of Norman Whitfield's "Ball of Confusion." During the eighties, she made the albums *Private Dancer*, *Break Every Rule*, and *Foreign Affair*, which sold millions of copies worldwide and yielded such hit singles as "The Best" and "I Don't Wanna Lose You." She also appeared in the film *Mad Max Beyond the Thunderdome*, and scored a huge hit with its theme tune, "We Don't Need Another Hero." She was later the subject of the biopic *What's Love Got to Do With It*, which told the story of her fight for survival.

During the late sixties and early seventies, the Ike and Tina Turner Review toured Europe and the U.S. opening for the Rolling Stones. This exposure helped launch Turner's later solo career.

SARAH VAUGHAN

1 9 2 4 - 1 9 9 0

SASSY SARAH VAUGHAN was known as the "divine one" on account of her wonderfully rich voice. She had a warm tone, a wide vocal range, and her improvisations were always highly inventive and perfectly executed. Her memorable hits included "Make Yourself Comfortable," "Passing Strangers" (on which she duetted with Billy Eckstine), and "Broken-Hearted Melody." By the end of her career she was regarded, like Ella Fitzgerald, as one of the great jazz singers of the century.

Vaughan was born and raised in Newark, New Jersey, the daughter of musical parents. Her father, a carpenter, played the guitar, while her mother, a laundress, sang in the Newark Baptist Church choir. As a child, Vaughan sang in the choir and took piano lessons, also studying church organ. In 1942 she won a talent contest at Harlem's Apollo Theater singing "Body and Soul," and the following year, on the advice of Billy Eckstine, Earl "Fatha" Hines signed her to sing and play second piano with his big band. When Eckstine left Hines's band to set up his own, Vaughan joined him.

Some of the musicians in Hines's and Eckstine's bands went on to become leading names in bebop, and in her early days, Vaughan was associated with the movement, recording with both Charlie Parker and Dizzy Gillespie and establishing a reputation as a jazz singer. However, it was her pop hits and romantic ballads that brought her commercial success. Her first chart hit was "Make Yourself Comfortable" in 1954, and she followed it up with such classics as "Whatever Lola Wants" from the Broadway musical *Damn Yankees*, a version of Harry Belafonte's "Banana Boat Song," and "Broken-Hearted Melody," a million-seller in 1959.

She took a five-year break from music during the late sixties but returned in the early seventies with a new maturity and a deeper vocal range—allegedly because of her chain smoking. In the eighties, despite poor health, she continued to record and perform as a soloist both with small groups featuring only bass and drums, and with symphony orchestras, touring the world and cementing her international reputation as a performer.

Sarah Vaughan's first husband was trumpeter George Treadwell, whom she married in 1945. He became her manager and changed her image from that of a shy and timid singer into that of a glamorous star. Under his guidance, between 1945 and 1954 (this picture was taken in 1950), she established her reputation as "the divine one."

DIONNE WARWICK

b . 1 9 4 0

DIONNE WARWICK's smooth, subtle vocal style and elegant phrasing made her the perfect singer for Burt Bacharach and Hal David's sophisticated pop ballads of the sixties. She was one of the first black women to become a pop star, with a string of classy, mid-tempo songs that cut straight across the traditional divisions between black and white music. After her success during the sixties, Warwick made several more hit records, including "Heartbreaker," written and produced by Barry Gibb of the Bee Gees. Some of her early hits, such as "Anyone Who Had a Heart," have been recorded by other artists, but few versions match her originals.

Warwick was born in East Orange, New Jersey, into a family of talented female singers, including soul singer Thelma Houston and Cissy Houston of the vocal group the Sweet Inspirations. Her sister Dee Dee was also a singer, and her niece Whitney Houston later became an international star. As a child, Dionne sang gospel in the Drinkard Sisters before forming her own group the Gospelaires. As a music student, she earned money by singing back-up in New York studios, where she met Bacharach. He got her a recording deal with Scepter/Wand, whose acts included the Shirelles.

Warwick's debut single, "Don't Make Me Over," was an immediate success, and the Bacharach–David team went on to write many hits for her, including several classics such as "Walk on By," "I Say a Little Prayer," and "Do You Know the Way to San José." During this period, she notched up record sales of twelve million. In 1972 she teamed up with Motown's Holland–Dozier–Holland songwriting team, but with less success. Two years later, she had a number one hit with the Detroit Spinners, and went on to tour with Isaac Hayes. During the eighties, she continued to release albums, working with a number of producers including, once again, Bacharach and David.

OPPOSITE PAGE: *Dionne Warwick comes from a family of talented singers, including Thelma, Cissy, and Whitney Houston.*
RIGHT: *Warwick's smooth vocal style appealed worldwide.*

DINAH WASHINGTON

1 9 2 4 — 1 9 6 3

DINAH WASHINGTON, "THE QUEEN OF THE BLUES," was famous for her gutsy blues style, her gospel delivery, and her impressive voice control. She was one of the great stars of the fifties, singing all manner of pop, country, and blues songs for the R&B market, before breaking into the mainstream charts in 1959 with "What a Diff'rence a Day Makes." Washington was a singer so rooted in her own musical culture that she could lend class and style to songs from any genre. And like Billie Holiday, by whom she was greatly influenced, she had the ability to give all her songs her own unique interpretation. Her success paved the way for anther generation of singers such as Aretha Franklin and Esther Phillips.

Dinah Washington was born Ruth Lee Jones in Tuscaloosa, Alabama, and as a child, moved with her family to Chicago, where she sang and played piano in church. After winning a talent contest at the Regal Theater in Chicago, she started to sing in local nightclubs and went on to tour with the Sallie Martin Gospel Singers. She then heard Billie Holiday, and decided to revert to singing in cabarets. In 1942 she adopted her stage name of Dinah Washington and began to sing with Lionel Hampton's band. However, Hampton's recording company, Decca, was not interested in signing her even though white artists such as Kay Starr were starting to cover her songs. Instead, she made some recordings of blues numbers such as "Evil Gal Blues" and "Salty Papa Blues" with members of the Hampton band and signed a deal with Mercury. This proved extremely successful, and between 1949 and 1961, she had a big run of hits on the black charts, including a number one, "This Bitter Earth," in 1960, and two duets with Brook Benton, "Baby (You've Got What It Takes)" and "A Rockin' Good Way (to Mess Around and Fall in Love)." She also covered country songs such as Hank Williams's "Cold, Cold Heart."

From the mid-fifties on, she began to record mostly in a jazz style, picking great songs from the thirties such as "What a Diff'rence a Day Makes" and "September in the Rain." As her career developed, her audience grew, but her private life was not as successful. She had nine husbands, a temper that was hard to control, a fondness for alcohol, and a tendency to use either sleeping pills or diet pills. In 1963 she died accidentally after mixing alcohol with sleeping pills.

Dinah Washington pictured in a Mercury Records publicity shot in 1962.

BARRY WHITE

b. 1 9 4 4

BARRY WHITE created a disco sound during the seventies that was rhythmic yet relaxed, sexual yet romantic. A big man, he was credited as having the deepest voice in pop, and at one stage in his career, had only to open his mouth to speak for women to swoon in the aisles. With songs coated in sugary string arrangements from the Love Unlimited Orchestra, White took chocolate-box romance to the limit. Yet the production on his records was impressive, and his approach added a much-needed melodic sweetness to the disco music of the period. There was also more than a touch of humor to White's image as the ultimate love god, reminiscent of the excessive, almost surreal romanticism of fifties doo-wop groups such as the Penguins.

White was born in Galveston, Texas, but grew up in Los Angeles, where he played organ in church. He sang with a vocal group called the Upfronts, and then got a job as an arranger for a small record company. His first hit was in 1962 as keyboard player on Bob and Earl's hit single "Harlem Shuffle." He went on to become an A&R man, discovering such soul singers as Felice Taylor, who had a hit with "I Feel Love Coming On" in 1967, and Viola Wills, whose "I'm Gonna Get Along Without You Now" was a hit in 1979, before concentrating his energies on the career of Love Unlimited, a girl group that included Diana Taylor, Linda James, and her sister Glodean (later his wife). Their hit, "Walking in the Rain with the One I Love," featured White's voice speaking on the telephone.

White then began a career as a solo artist, using a novel style of intimate, romantic chat on his recordings. His first hit came in 1973 with a half-spoken, half-grunted "I'm Gonna Love You Just a Little More Baby." During the next few years such songs as "Never, Never Gonna Give Ya Up," "Can't Get Enough of Your Love, Babe," and "You're the First, the Last, My Everything" were hugely popular and sold millions of copies, as did his production of "Love's Theme," an instrumental number one hit for the Love Unlimited Orchestra.

He disappeared from the scene during the early eighties, but returned in 1987 and found an affectionate audience for his unique brand of romantic music who helped sustain his career for a number of years. His latest hit came in 1992 when he duetted with Lisa Stansfield on a new version of her song "All Around the World."

In the seventies, Barry White's unique brand of "smooch disco" sold millions worldwide.

BOBBY WOMACK

b . 1 9 4 4

BOBBY WOMACK is significant in black music as "the last soul man"—the last soul performer to sing, write, and tour in the tradition of sixties' soul singers such as Sam Cooke, Otis Redding, Wilson Pickett, Solomon Burke, and Joe Tex. Through sheer talent and commitment, Womack became one of the few soul artists of his generation to survive the advent of funk and disco. During the seventies and eighties, he consistently upheld the values of songwriting at a time when strong production—rather than strong songs and singers—had come to dominate the market. For this reason, Womack is widely respected as the guardian of a classic soul tradition that, since the sixties, has gone through periods of being unfashionable but which continues to survive more ephemeral trends in black music.

ABOVE: *Womack's 1981 album* The Poet *is thought by many to be his best.*

Born in Cleveland, Ohio, Bobby's father formed his sons Cecil, Curtis, Harry, Friendly, and Bobby into a gospel quartet known as the Valentinos. The brothers toured with Sam Cooke, and when Cooke crossed over from gospel into the pop mainstream, the Valentinos followed, signing to Cooke's Sar label. In 1964 Bobby co-wrote "It's All Over Now," later covered by the Rolling Stones. When Cooke died, the group split. Bobby married Cooke's widow and worked as a session guitarist. He wrote such hits as "I'm a Midnight Mover" for Wilson Pickett and then launched a solo career. He recorded for a number of labels until he settled at United Artists in the early seventies, where he made the albums *Communication* and *Understanding* as well as a collection of country songs entitled *BW Goes CW*.

In 1981, after a dip in his career partly caused by drug problems, he made what many consider his best album, *The Poet*. Successive albums such as *The Poet II*, *Womagic*, and *The Last Soul Man* established him as a true soul survivor, a position that he maintains today. His last album, *Resurrection*, released in 1994, achieved good sales and proved that his creativity has not left him.

OPPOSITE PAGE: *Despite an uneven start to his solo career, Womack kept writing and playing.*

STEVIE WONDER

b . 1 9 5 0

STEVIE WONDER HAS earned his place as an icon of black music not only because of his extraordinary musical talent but also because of his role as an elder statesman within it. For over three decades, he has made music that has ranged from classic love songs such as "For Once in My Life" and "Isn't She Lovely" to such inventive, exploratory albums as *Music of My Mind*, on which he played all the instruments.

He began as a child prodigy at Motown, and later became the first Motown artist to gain complete control over his financial and artistic career. This gave him the freedom to respond to new trends in music, and during the seventies, he pioneered the use of synthesizers, linking soul music with the rock mainstream. Between 1963 and 1986, he had over fifty hit singles and over twenty hit albums, and remains one of the best-loved entertainers in show business. During the eighties, he successfully campaigned to make Martin Luther King's birthday a national holiday in America, sponsoring two marches in Washington and writing the song "Happy Birthday," which reached the Top 5 in 1985. He has also spoken out against nuclear war, taken part in campaigns to stop drink driving, and sponsored an eye disease research and care facility.

Steveland Morris was born in Saginaw, Michigan, a premature baby who was given too much oxygen in his incubator, causing him to become blind for life. By age eight, he had learned to play piano, harmonica, and percussion, and at age ten, Berry Gordy signed him to Motown, naming him Little Stevie Wonder. In 1963 Wonder's fourth single, "Fingertips Part II," which featured his harmonica playing, reached number one on the pop charts. Simultaneously, his debut album, *The Twelve Year Old Genius*, topped the album charts. Hits such as "Uptight," "My Cherie Amour," and "Signed, Sealed, Delivered I'm Yours" followed, until in 1971 he set up his own production company, worked on his synthesizers, and came up with his second number one hit, "Superstition." Great albums including *Talking Book*, *Innervisions*, *Fulfillingness First Finale*, and *Songs in the Key of Life* followed, all of which yielded hit singles. In the eighties and nineties, Wonder continued to record successfully, responding to new movements such as rap, as well as producing other artists.

Stevie Wonder's musical career has spanned the last forty years of the twentieth century. During the sixties, he was a child prodigy; during the seventies, he was at the cutting edge of funk; and from the eighties onward, he was an international superstar.

LESTER YOUNG

1 9 0 9 — 1 9 5 9

IN THE THIRTIES, Lester Young became the most influential tenor saxophone player in jazz. His playing departed from the full-bodied sound of Coleman Hawkins, up to then the leading tenor, and introduced a streamlined, melodic style that was relaxed, graceful, and rhythmic. Young's impact was immense: his style laid the foundations for a new generation of modern jazz artists such as Charlie Parker, Stan Getz, and John Coltrane. During his career, apart from his solo work, Young's most notable accomplishments were with Count Basie's band and with Billie Holiday, who called him "Prez" (short for President).

Young was born in Woodville, Mississippi. As a child, he toured the carnivals of the Midwest, playing drums in his parents' family band. He then took up the tenor saxophone, and after traveling around the country playing in different bands, moved to Kansas City to join Count Basie. He left Basie's band to join Fletcher Henderson's, replacing Coleman Hawkins, but his very different style was not appreciated, and after a few months, he returned to playing with Basie. With members of Basie's band and producer John Hammond, Young went on to record classic tracks such as "Shoe Shine Boy," "Lady Be Good," and "Lester Leaps In." It was these recordings that brought him to the notice of the wider public and of other musicians, who were impressed by his smooth, legato phrasing. During this time, he also accompanied Billie Holiday, forming a lasting musical and emotional bond with her.

In 1944 he completed a short film for Warner Bros, *Jamming the Blues*, which was nominated for an Academy Award the following year. Just after the filming was finished, Young was drafted into the U.S. Army, which proved a bruising experience for him. A sensitive, introspective man, he suffered constant ill health and was imprisoned for smoking marijuana. "It was a nightmare—one mad nightmare," he said. "They sent me down to Georgia—and that was enough to make me blow my top." He left the army and resumed recording in 1945. His first session, in Los Angeles, resulted in the sublime album *These Foolish Things*. In the late forties, he continued to perform and record as a freelance soloist, but took to drink, which further impaired his health. He died as a result of a heart attack at age fifty, only a few months before the death of his friend Billie Holiday.

Lester Young performing on stage in New York in 1944.

INDEX